BUILDING BEAUTIFUL: CLASSICAL HOUSES BY JOHN SIMPSON

BUILDING BEAUTIFUL

CLASSICAL HOUSES BY JOHN SIMPSON

CLIVE ASLET

New York · Paris · London · Milan

This book is dedicated to my wife, Erica,
my sons, Nicholas and Alexander,
and my darling daughter, Antonia
—J. S.

TABLE OF CONTENTS

FOREWORD BY JOHN SIMPSON
8

INTRODUCTION
14

I. PALAZZO GRIMANI, VENICE
28

II. BELSIZE PARK, LONDON
76

III. HAREWELL HALL, WHERWELL, HAMPSHIRE
112

IV. ASHFOLD HOUSE, EAST SUSSEX
150

V. 29 GREAT JAMES STREET, BLOOMSBURY
186

VI. CONCLUSION
204

VII. POSTSCRIPT BY JOHN SIMPSON
212

ACKNOWLEDGMENTS
220

FOREWORD BY JOHN SIMPSON

Our homes are the closest we come to creating an ideal and beautiful world for ourselves. An intimate space that is our very own, convenient and secure but above all a place that affords us comfort and joy. Home is a sanctuary to which we retire to relax surrounded by all the things that make us happy and remind us of the places and people that we enjoy. It is a repository where we keep mementos of the events and achievements that define our lives and the objects to which, for one reason or another, we have become so intimately attached.

Proposal for a new office building on Lime Street in the City of London seen through the arch of Leadenhall Market. (Painting by Carl Laubin.)

It is also the name we give to the place that we grow up in or where we raise a family. It reflects our roots, the world that belongs to us, the values that we identify with that set us apart from those around us. It defines our cultural and aesthetic preferences, the lifestyle we are accustomed to and the habits that have become the ritual of our daily lives.

Inevitably the organization and form of a house are not there simply to provide shelter and security but to facilitate a lifestyle that we have chosen for ourselves and for those around us. The location of a dining room at the center of a house for instance will inevitably determine how often a family will share a meal around a table rather than just snack in the kitchen or eat individually while watching television. Similarly a home arranged around a series of separate rooms will allow family members to enjoy different activities that would be incompatible otherwise in one open-plan space, with one listening to or playing a musical instrument while another is quietly meditating or reading a book in another. This way the arrangement and physical nature of the house sets the criteria by which we live. It determines the ritual which, in all probability, is the single most predictable constant of our daily existence. It provides comfort during difficult times and the backdrop against which we bring up and educate our children.

Despite putting such store by our privacy, we are nevertheless social beings. We are never happy to be in complete isolation and a home that has an outlook with views over its surroundings is highly prized and particularly so when combined with a garden or even just a simple balcony or small outside terrace. We all want to feel we belong and connected to the things around us and especially so to the natural world,

which is so often vital to our sense of wellbeing, health and sanity. That is why a home where the level of sunlight inside can keep us aware of the time of day and the weather outside can be so much more satisfying as a place to live. A conservatory with palms, a loggia with vines or a balcony cascading with plants bridges the divide with the world outside. Such an architectural device celebrates this transition and extends the period that we enjoy with the flowers, birds even the insects and bees who become, for a few months at least, an extended family of friends with whom we are pleased to share our home.

Residential housing designed by John Simpson for Poundbury, outside Dorchester, U. K., following a master plan commissioned by the Prince of Wales from Léon Krier.

Most of us also enjoy having other people into our homes and love to entertain our family and friends. As a result, our houses need to be capable occasionally of transformation from small, cozy spaces that an intimate group might enjoy, to a suitable venue for a birthday or Christmas party. This is where the architecture and design play their part—providing the connections and sequence of rooms that through strategically placed openings, mirrors and devices such as screens and double doors that can be drawn together and dramatically opened up—to conjure, as if by magic, an impression of a large space in which we can welcome our guests with appropriate theater and ceremony.

Although it is often said that a person is judged by the company they keep, a brief visit to their home will reveal so much more about them; their interests and preferences, their values and aspirations as well their attitude and philosophy to life. This is why admitting someone into that inner sanctum of home will always be such a significant gesture of friendship and affection.

For an architect, designing your own home is an opportunity to explore ideas that you have been itching to try out and do so without the necessity of convincing a client of their merit or having to find ways to weave them into a strictly controlled budget. You have no one except yourself and perhaps your family to account to. Moreover, every home is subject to pressure. There is always a need for more bookshelves or space for a new piece of furniture or a place to hang another picture, not to mention that new extension, conservatory or swimming pool. For me, working on my own houses I have

been able to afford the time to be more than usually thoughtful and disciplined and yet at the same time philosophical, playful and even whimsical. There has been lots of scope to design to an intricate level and to discover new ways of exploiting available and emerging technology. It has given me the opportunity to fine-tune techniques I have used later in my professional career, using architecture to imply a chronology or history of how it has come about and weave a story around the reality of the building or to emphasize the otherwise insignificant or make something look more substantial and imposing than it really is. It has been a testing ground for interiors and furniture that I have been able to live with before developing for clients on other projects. It has given me the backdrop and stage to display the objects and artifacts that I have collected and a place where I can enjoy the company of friends. Most of all it has defined the world in which my wife, Erica, and I have brought up our children, Nicholas, Alexander and Antonia, and has given us many cherished memories. It has provided a firm, confident and optimistic foundation from which the next generation can step forward into the world outside.

Development along Old Church Street, Chelsea, by John Simpson. View looking north along Church Street showing the new terraced buildings designed to follow the original historic building line. The first six buildings in the foreground are all new. This urban design scheme provides three new terraced houses, four cottages, 22 flats, a new vicarage and a new church hall.

11

INTRODUCTION

This book is about the domestic world of John Simpson. John is an architect, the son of
an architect: he grew up in the certainty that his life would always be in architecture.
As the Prince of Wales observed in the foreword to an earlier book, he has built schools, art
galleries, recital halls, hotels, university buildings, chapels, museums, libraries, gymnasia,
a debating chamber and a military rehabilitation center for
seriously wounded servicemen and women. In New York, he
has been responsible for the first fully Classical building for
half a century. But at the center of his life are his homes.

The new Carhart building by John Simpson at
the junction of 5th Avenue and 95th Street in
Manhattan, New York. It was described by the
New York Landmarks Commission as the first
truly Classical building to have been built in the
City since the 1930s.

For John is not only interested in architecture as a
public art but in the shape, form, use and decoration of the
rooms that lie inside his buildings. Conjuror-like, he magics usable space out of places
that other architects might neglect or fail to notice, creating drama as he does so.
He designs furniture as well as facades. These talents come together in the places that
he shares with his wife, Erica, and in which his three children, Nicholas, Alexander
and Antonia, grew up. Like the family, the spaces have evolved over the years. They
have also grown in number, with a restored palazzo in Venice and Hampshire residence
complementing the London home, which has itself evolved out of the single flat that
he and Erica bought in Belsize Park in 1980, and his practice's office in Bloomsbury.

John has always designed. At Marlborough College, he made a desk for his study,
incorporating an old valve radio that had belonged to his grandfather; the aerial was a
wire, borrowed from the Combined Cadet Force, which stretched halfway across the
adjacent games pitch. In religious education lessons, he designed a church. Whereas
other alumni from Marlborough went on to pursue academic courses at university,
he chose the Bartlett School of Architecture (part of University College London).
He arrived in 1972, to begin a course lasting, as is usual with architecture, seven years.

Le Corbusier, once a god, was now dead, and so—at the Bartlett—was his
reputation. In the wider world, this was still the age of Brutalism: Alison and Peter
Smithson's Robin Hood Gardens opened in 1972, the National Theatre in 1977.
But the Bartlett was in the grip of other passions. At its head was Llewellyn Davies,

an architect who built hospitals and surrounded himself with technocrats, whose expertise was in the provision of services. But in what was still the hippie era there was also a more radical element on the teaching staff, committed to the construction of eco dwellings out of recycled materials such as old car tires. Their ideal of a sustainable architecture, which would leave a light footprint on the planet, now looks ahead of its time. Then, for all its good intentions, it had an aura of eccentricity, made visible in teachers such as the White Rabbit, who lived in a self-built shack in Epping Forest, surviving on food grown by himself and wearing a motley of home-made or second-hand clothes. John was left to find his own way. There was little teaching of relevance to his own passion, which was for Classicism.

Pitzhanger Manor by Sir John Soane at Ealing, London. Originally built by Soane as a family house for himself and his family between 1800 and 1804.

Classicism in Britain was at such a low ebb that many people thought it had expired altogether. The tradition had lost its vigor in the interwar years, just as it was being challenged by the new ideology of Modernism. Modernism swept the board after 1945. Classical architects survived, like the despised ministrants to an old-fashioned and discredited faith, on the meager pickings provided by country-house work, as the aristocracy retreated from the big house to a smaller one or the stables. Raymond Erith, the most distinguished of these architects, died in 1973; his partner Quinlan Terry had yet to achieve the fame that descended on him in the 1980s, with the design of Richmond Riverside. But John had one mentor (albeit dead) to whom he could turn for guidance and inspiration: Sir John Soane.

Sir John Soane's Museum in Lincoln's Inn Fields is a twenty-minute walk from the Bartlett, through the Georgian terraced streets and squares of Bloomsbury. It was preserved under his will exactly as he had left it at his death in 1837. Soane meant it to be used as an object of study by young architects: John (incidentally his namesake) must have been exactly the sort of person he had in mind—although Soane could hardly have imagined the direction that architecture would have taken in the mid twentieth century. The house is full of collections, including the drawings from Robert Adam's office. Hogarth's *A Rake's Progress* and other paintings were

displayed on a space-saving arrangement of folding panels, which, in those distant days, you could operate yourself, without even wearing white gloves. Antique fragments, casts of sculpture, and cork models had been assembled not only for their intrinsic interest but also as teaching aids for Soane's lectures at the Royal Academy and the instruction he gave his pupils. Soane worked from home; his assistants' desks stood on a platform, suspended amid his treasures.

The tribune known as the Dome Room at Lincoln's Inn Fields, London, at the Sir John Soane Museum in London built from 1792–1825 by Soane as his London house after selling Pitzhanger Manor. He collected fragments of ancient buildings, which he arranged in the museum to use to teach his students about the sculptural aspects of architecture. (Engraving by Mason Jackson of the sarcophagus of Seti I in the Sepulchral Chamber, as shown in the *Illustrated London News* in 1864.)

But the Soane Museum is about more than collections. There is drama in the contrasts of scale. There is ingenuity in the manipulation of space. There are seductive effects of light, shining from hidden sources or filtered through colored glass. All these qualities are expressed in a building which tugs and stretches the Classical tradition to find new ways of using old forms, with half an eye always being kept on the origins of Classicism (as Soane believed) in primitive construction; ornament is pared away to a bare roll of molding or an incised line. Architecture is reduced to its essence. John imbibed these ideas on his many visits. He says that the Soane Museum taught him, above all, about scale. Here was a house packed full of excitement, in terms of architectural ideas; but it remained forever a comfortable and elegant home. Soane is the starting point for many of the homes in this book.

In his years out from the Bartlett, John worked for John Worthington of DEGW, turning a brick Victorian Gothic church into the Jackson Lane Community Centre, with theater and basketball court: a job that would prepare him for working with old buildings and traditional materials. He established his own practice as soon as he left the school in 1979. What a year to do so. The 1970s had not only been terrible for British architecture but for Britain as a whole, which some people called the Sick Man of Europe. Structural problems in the economy were compounded by the Oil Crisis of 1973, which had a particular consequence for domestic architecture: with the doubling of the oil price, big country houses became impossible to heat. Strikes

were incessant, inflation soared, investment withered, and the Heath government's attempt to face down the National Union of Mineworkers led to power cuts and the imposition of a three-day week; a general election fought on the slogan "Who Governs Britain?" led to the government's defeat. The culmination of these woes was the Winter of Discontent in 1978–79 when a program of public sector strikes left rubbish uncollected and the dead unburied. Under Mrs. Thatcher, Britain would recover its sense of purpose— but that would only happen after two years of recession and a Bank of England interest rate of 17 percent. It was a dire time for a young architect to enter the profession.

Fortunately, John's family were sympathetic. His parents John and Lydia could give him a job: a small, almost pocket-sized country house for their own use in Sussex. This was Ashfold House, an essay in the style of Soane, not large in scale but full to the brim with architectural ideas, the drawings lovingly worked and reworked as only those of a first project can be. Compact buildings can be harder for the architect than bigger ones, where the tolerances are greater: minor inaccuracies may barely be noticed in a large space but become glaringly obvious in a confined space. As John puts it, "the practice started with all guns blazing," being responsible for the creation of everything in the house, including an interior scheme that included Simpson-designed furniture and curtains. The style of the furniture was influenced by Regency arbiter of taste, Thomas Hope.

There was a practical reason for bespoke furniture at Ashfold: genuine Regency pieces would have been too big for the small rooms. John's solution was to design furniture that either saved space through being built-in or was of slightly miniaturized dimensions. In those days, brown furniture was still—*O tempora! O mores!*—aspirational and expensive; specially commissioned pieces were a better value. Beyond these utilitarian concerns was the pleasure it gave. Here were bravura interiors, created for an age that was hardly used to such élan—and on a scale that

only added to the wonder. It is a triumph of *magnum in parvo*, which, in a book of that title, the eighteenth-century architect William Halfpenny called the marrow of architecture. In Ashfold, we can see what he meant.

And the taste that this gave John for controlling every aspect of an interior has never left him. It has resurfaced not only in the homes seen in this book but, notably, his Soane-inspired reorganizing of Gonville and Caius College, Cambridge, which has given to the world a stackable version of the ancient Greek klismos chair: cast aluminum backs, patinated to look like bronze, provide the necessary strength.

For a long time it was John's only built project and a showpiece for the nascent Classical Revival that was trumpeted in two small but important exhibitions at the Building Centre in London's Store Street: *Classical Revival, Classical Survival* in 1984 and *Real Architecture* in 1987. The idea had been that *Classical Revival*, dreamt up by John and a few architectural friends, would be held in his office. Word reached them, however, that the Greater London Council,

(left) The new Lord Colyton Room at Gonville and Caius College, Cambridge, by John Simpson. The interior of this room was created by converting the old Munro library of 1917, which itself was inserted within the original shell of the great hall built in the first half of the fifteenth century. It is based on a design by Sir John Soane for the hall erected in 1792 and demolished by Anthony Salvin in 1853, when the current hall was built. The room is now used as a combination room for the fellows at the college.
(above) Sitting Room at Ashfold House in Sussex. The interior furniture and furnishings in both rooms including the carpet in the Lord Colyton Room were also designed by John Simpson.

under its radical chairman Ken Livingstone, was awarding grants for arts projects—and they were regarded as sufficiently subversive to get one of £500. It was enough for the exhibition to be mounted at the Building Centre in Store Street. As yet, the amount of built work that could be shown was modest. Quinlan Terry was the most established; his practice, once sustained largely by the design of garden buildings and country-house alterations, had begun to gather pace—and the opprobrium of the architectural establishment—by attracting commissions for both larger country houses and office buildings. Robert Adam, Alireza Sagharchi, Jeremy Blake, Julian Bicknell and John himself were starting out. The show was bulked out by contributions from an old guard of traditionalists, including the Arts and Crafts architect John Brandon-Jones and the Gothicist Stephen Dykes Bower. Reports appeared in some

of the better newspapers and by the standards of the Building Centre—admittedly unambitious—it attracted an extraordinary number of visitors. A second exhibition on the same theme called *Real Architecture* was staged in 1987. So unfamiliar was the Classical vocabulary that the Roman numerals on the front of the catalogue read: "MCMLXXXVIII—1988." Still, the exhibitions were enough to suggest that Britain's small band of Classicists, far from being, as critics sought to present them, a group of misfits and oddballs, were forming a movement.

Ashfold led to another commission: a country house for the king and queen of Jordan. Although this was glamorous, the nature of the client meant that it would never be published. But the Building Centre exhibitions had the public's attention, with important consequences. One came in a request from the Prince of Wales to visit *Real Architecture*. Prince Charles had already infuriated the architectural establishment by using his address to the hundred and fiftieth anniversary dinner of the Royal Institute of British Architects to criticize the profession's aloofness and unpopularity. The designs then being proposed for an extension to the National Gallery were likened to a "monstrous carbuncle on the face of a much-loved and elegant friend." *Real Architecture* helped develop his ideas. Having been initially attracted to community architecture, he now segued toward Classicism. He was ever afterwards a powerful champion for the cause.

A series of lectures that John organized for *Real Architecture* introduced him to another standard-bearer: David Watkin, then a lecturer in the history of art at the University of Cambridge, where he would later become a professor. They had a common interest in Thomas Hope, whose biography David had written. David soon became a friend. Convinced that Classicism was an appropriate style for the modern age, David used his influence on John's behalf whenever the opportunity offered;

(above left) View of the proposed development at Paternoster Square next to St Paul's Cathedral in the City of London showing the new buildings around the square together with the new market hall and St Paul's Cathedral in the background (painting by Carl Laubin). With the support of the Prince of Wales the purpose of this masterplan was to show how a traditional approach to design can provide commercially viable buildings whilst creating a better and more attractive neighborhood within the city. *(above right)* View looking into McCrum Yard at Eton College by John Simpson, toward the new museum and debating chamber. A fountain forms the centerpiece to the quadrangle, which provides cooling for the hall using a process of evaporative cooling.

22

two years before his death in 2018, David's four decades of advocacy culminated in *The Architecture of John Simpson*, published by Rizzoli. It was through David that Simpson was introduced to the Cambridge colleges of Gonville and Caius and Peterhouse, at both of which he executed major schemes.

The late 1980s were years of battle. At the end of 1987, the Prince of Wales spoke against the modernist redevelopment proposed for Paternoster Square, immediately beside St. Paul's Cathedral. The next day, John, backed by the *Evening Standard*, submitted a counter planning application (planning applications can be submitted independent of owning the land). Two years later, after the site had changed hands, John's scheme was accepted in principle, although other, more

(above left and right) Loggia of cast-iron and glass designed by John Simpson for a new garden for the public on the east front of Kensington Palace. The floral ornament of the loggia combines happily with gilded repeats of the royal cypher, E II R, below the crown. The palace was repopened by Her Majesty The Queen in March 2012 as part of her jubilee celebrations.

23

experienced architects, were asked to design the buildings. About the same time, John was at work on a new village, radically designed—by the standards of the time—to be somewhere that people actually wanted to live. Old villages, John saw, were attractive because of the variety achieved through their long evolution. At Upper Donnington, he sought to achieve a similar effect by designing a tight inner core around a broad, tree-lined street—almost a marketplace. To one side, a formal crescent curled around an amphitheater—as it were, an addition of the mid-Georgian period; while more spacious, less formal streets formed the fringes of the village, as though a Regency promoter had come along and built terraces in about 1820. This was picturesque and revolutionary. Alas, Upper Donnington failed to obtain planning permission because it lay outside the area scheduled by Newbury District Council for development.

The 1990s saw John contribute a market building and several streets of mostly yellow brick to the Duchy of Cornwall's Poundbury development outside Dorchester, a project of the Prince of Wales. Another royal commission came with the Queen's Gallery, Buckingham Palace, which opened in 2002. Outside, a temple portico, entered from two directions and therefore designed to look as imposing from the side as the front, was formed from stout Greek Doric columns. This gave into an entrance

EN COMMÉMORATION
DE
L'EXPOSITION
DE LONDRES
1851

The new Propylaeum for the Queen's Gallery at Buckingham Palace

hall, grandly decorated with a program of figurative sculpture by Alexander Stoddart. A splendid double staircase, enriched with a bronze balustrade, to which bronze ropes and tassels to reduce—in case of children wanting to put their heads through—the spaces between the uprights, in line with building regulations, leads up to the galleries, the last of which was part of the scheme designed in the Regency period by John Nash. Recent triumphs have included a new "yard" or court for Eton College, a new hospital—the Defense and National Rehabilitation Centre—attached to a country house, and a reimagining of the Royal College of Music opposite the Albert Hall. None of these projects, be it noted, is a country house. Classicism has moved beyond the ghetto that it occupied when John started practice.

(left) The new entrance hall at The Queen's Gallery at Buckingham Palace by John Simpson. It is designed to remind visitors entering the building of the origins of Western Art and Architecture. Columns derived from sixth-century B. C. Doric temples at Paestum are combined with a newly commissioned sculptural frieze by Alexander Stoddard depicting the Queen's reign through allegorical scenes from the Iliad and the Odyssey, the earliest known works of literature in Western Art.
(above) Elevation of the new propylaeum designed by John Simpson for the Queen's Gallery at Buckingham Palace.

And yet domestic architecture remains, as this book will reveal, intensely important to him, not least when it comes to the homes for his own family. When John and Erica married in 1980, they bought—as is natural, or was then—their first flat. It showed their priorities: the ground floor of a substantial stucco-fronted house in Belsize Park, with two grand rooms (which would become grander still before very long) for entertaining. Over the years, this has expanded as adjacent flats came on the market, to be incorporated, with characteristic ingenuity, into a single dwelling. To Belsize Park has been added an eighteenth-century palace in Venice, gloriously restored, and a thatched country house that might have developed in many stages since the monastic period—had not John in fact designed the whole of it from scratch in the twenty-first century.

The result is not merely a visual feast but an object lesson in how to live well. Let's fling open the doors. The music has started. I think I see John there, offering a glass of champagne.

I

PALAZZO GRIMANI, VENICE

In 2016, John and Erica Simpson acquired what, to many people, is the cynosure of civilized existence: an apartment—an entire palace, as it would have been when it was built in the seventeenth century—in Venice. Their restoration has been breathtaking. Only those who know what it was like during its previous incarnation, as the Bridge Club of Venice, can appreciate the extent of the transformation. Who could have guessed that a largely complete eighteenth-century scheme of decoration lay hidden beneath the layers of nicotine, paint, parquet and yellow silk? Nobody. But fortune has favored the bold.

Palazzo Grimani. The main saloon on the piano nobile. The building was restored for residential use having been used as the Venice Bridge Club since 1964. The transcenae screens were introduced as part of the new scheme.

The palazzo was one of many Venice properties owned by the Grimani family, patricians who had been prominent in the life of the city since the Renaissance; they produced three doges, two cardinals and two bishops. By water, it is only a few minutes from St. Mark's Square, next to the Gritti Palace hotel. In Venetian terms, this is a relatively elevated spot, a full three feet above St. Mark's Square, as can be seen at *acqua alta*: when St. Mark's Square is knee-deep in water, it only licks the doorstep of the Palazzo Grimani, so that the *magazzino*—ground floor used for storage—remains dry.

There is no canal frontage but the principal facade gives onto an extension of the Campo di Santa Maria del Giglio—*giglio* meaning lily: a reference both to the flower traditionally carried by the archangel Gabriel at the Annunciation and, presumably, the heraldic lily often used on Venetian coats of arms. This church was originally—and still often is—known as Santa Maria Zobenigo, after the Jubanico family who built it in the ninth century; the change of name dates from the rebuilding after the death of Antonio Barbaro, a *capitan del mar* and governor of what was then the Venetian Empire, in 1679. Barbaro and his family feature prominently on the white marble facade, to the almost complete exclusion of religious imagery.

In the 1730s, Canaletto depicted the church and square in a painting now in the Wrightsman Collection at the Metropolitan Museum in New York. It shows the Palazzo Grimani as a building of only two stories, rather than the present four;

in a city where land was at a premium, palazzi were often built at two stories, then heightened with the addition of a second piano nobile accordingly to need—for example, to house children as they grew older. Today, the facade is covered in light yellow stucco (Canaletto shows it as red); in the center of the piano nobile is an arcade of six Ionic columns made of white stone, with a further two round-headed windows to each side. When built, the palace had a shallow pantile roof, above which rise tall chimneys of typical Venetian type, on tall semi-external flues; the inverted cones in which they end were originally intended as a precaution against hot cinders in a densely packed city, vulnerable to destructive fires. Although the roof and chimneys have now gone, in all other respects the palazzo is that now owned by the Simpsons.

Santa Maria Zobenigo showing Palazzo Grimani on the left as it was at the time when the painting was done by Canaletto for Joseph Smith (ca. 1674–1770), British consul in Venice from 1744 to 1760. The original palazzo was two stories high and was painted in the classic Venetian terracotta color. It was built by the family probably for pleasure as a casino when gambling in the city was formalized in 1638 with its first gambling house.

The date of construction is not known. Inside, the earliest surviving plasterwork, a scheme of flowers and panels in which the color is contained in the plaster itself, can be dated, stylistically, to around 1700. In the nineteenth century, the palace was raised to its present height, when two additional stories were added. At this time, the double-height entrance hall, which probably contained an imperial staircase, was divided vertically into two spaces, each with its own staircase, making the upper part of the building independent of the lower. There is some question as to whether the palazzo actually functioned as a palace. The reason for the doubt comes in the fretwork panels separating an intermediate level space from the principal rooms. Clearly it was intended that the latter should be overlooked. One suggestion is that the building served as a casino (Venetian word) where gambling could take place. In the early Venetian Republic, gambling had been outlawed on pain of various horrific punishments; however, the battle against this popular aristocratic pastime was lost in the seventeenth century—in 1638, in the *Ridotto* or private room attached to the Doge's Palace. It is tempting to think that the Palazzo Grimani was built soon afterwards.

A casino for gambling might have provided a useful source of income for the Grimanis, who, like other Venetian families, had diversified from trade and the Church into theaters (they owned several). An intermediate floor, or mezzanine, must also have served as a minstrels' gallery to the present dining room, since it is clear that this was intended for music. In 1964, the building continued its connection with cards, although of a more cerebral nature, by becoming home to the *Circolo Bridge di Venezia* (the Bridge Club of Venice), which updated the décor—not too destructively, as it would turn out—by laying new floors, putting up wall coverings and applying coats of paint.

When the Simpsons arrived, the pale gray marbling of the pilasters that line the drawing room, the pinks and greens of the plaster panels and the blues of the door had been emulsioned over. Once the paint layers were picked off, the original colors were revealed in a state of almost miraculous freshness. This scheme appears to be in the Venetian equivalent of the 1790s Directoire style, only with plasterwork that seems not completely to have forgotten the Rococo.

Half a century of cigarette smoking by bridge players had turned the ceiling to a chestnut brown; this has now been removed. If this ceiling was once painted with an allegorical scene, like that in the dining room, the work is now lost. Cameos of what appear to be Caesars occupy the overdoors. The cameos at the edges of the ceiling were replaced in the nineteenth century with images of what was then the family living here—father, mother and two children.

As found, the floors throughout the apartment had been laid with parquet. Against all advice (why would parquet have been laid if the floor beneath were not thoroughly rotten?), the Simpsons lifted it, to find terrazzo of some magnificence. Terrazzo is the traditional floor covering of marble chips set in lime mortar, polished smooth, oiled and repolished. In the drawing room, the effect is that of a nougat of plum, black, white, gray and yellow stones, some of them being fossiliferous and bigger than are conventionally used in making terrazzo these days.

Much of the furniture in the room has been made from designs that John Simpson has drawn over the years. The fabrics have been digitally printed to provide bespoke patterns at a fraction of what weaving would cost. The chandelier—or electrolier—dates from the arrival of the bridge club, the 1960s; since the scale is right, the Simpsons were anxious to keep it, missing pieces being reproduced by craftsmen on Murano. The grand piano was shipped from England—at a considerable cost to the nerves of Erica Simpson, who accompanied it: the final stages of the journey being made by motor barge, then a caterpillar-tracked crawler machine to take it upstairs.

In terms of surviving decoration, the pièce de résistance is the dining room. One color note is set by the floor: the largest panel is Sienna yellow, set into a border that mirrors that of the ceiling. A second comes from the powder blue of the doors. Around the walls, trophies of molded plaster, nearly all showing musical instruments—with an appropriate nod, in one of the smaller trophies, to Architecture—hang from swagged garlands. Set in a gilded frame, the centerpiece of the ceiling shows Apollo surrounded by allegorical maidens—dancing with a tambourine, writing music and blowing a trumpet—while cupids descend with a crown of laurels (presumably to supplement the one that Apollo already wears). The style is that of Tiepolo, the likely artist being one of his pupils, Costantino Cedini. To each side of the ceiling are tablets of putti, apparently representing the seasons, although time has made them too dark to read.

32

(left top to bottom) An eighteenth-century canape recovered with specially designed fabric and sketches for new furniture by John Simpson for Palazzo Grimani in Venice.

The modern chandelier, bought in London, does not disassemble; it therefore had to be transported from London on a cradle, housed within a metal drum. While the double doors at the bottom of the palazzo were wide enough to receive it, the chandelier could not fit through the door of the apartment itself. Fortunately, it was susceptible to being squeezed into a thinner volume, before being opened out again, when fitted into position.

The guest bedroom and bathroom contain an earlier scheme of painted decoration. The bed here is a mahogany four-poster with painted canopy, draped in swags of blue silk. On the walls are two paintings that seemed enormous when viewed in London but fit elegantly into a room of such height. One is a Neoclassical sybil, while the other depicts Abraham sacrificing Isaac.

In matters of conservation, Italian ways are different from those in London, and the watery circumstances of Venice add a further complication. After contracts were exchanged, it took a year for completion to be achieved: the vendor had forgotten to obtain the change of use from bridge club to dwelling, or to inform his sister, who co-owned the property, of the proposed sale. But such glitches have now been forgotten. The ugly duckling that the Simpsons found when they bought the Palazzo Grimani is now one of the serenest swans, in a city famous for serenity.

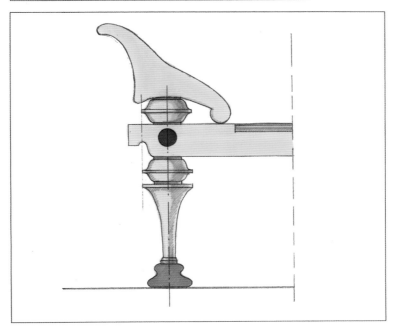

34

The main central saloon at Palazzo Grimani.
The interior scheme originates from the early
nineteenth century and was restored by removing
white and yellow emulsion paint to reveal the
original colors. The piano is a 1905 D-type
Steinway made in Steinway's New York workshop
and suitably embellished with swags. The chair
to the right of the piano is a Caesar and is a John
Simpson variation on Lutyens's Napoleon chair.

The furniture made from mahogany by P&S joinery in Suffolk was specially designed by John Simpson for this room based on Roman precedents. The chandelier is an old Murano one made in the 1950s. The carpet was bought in England and is one of a limited edition made by Axminster Heritage in 2005. In keeping with the eighteenth-century tradition, it was paraded through the town when completed and taken to the church to be blessed. Only five were made, one of which is at Clarence House in London.

The fabric for the upholstery was specially designed and printed using digital techniques. The eighteenth-century canape on the left of the picture came from the Duchess of Roxburghe's sale at Christie's and was recovered with specially designed fabric printed specifically for the purpose. The anthemeon and oroboros woven into the design of the fabric are heraldic devices from the family coat of arms.

Saloon looking through to the main bedroom. The side tables are designed to match the upholstered furniture. The design incorporates the characteristic Roman *lentil* shaped moldings to support what looks like a bowl that forms the top of the table. The same lentil-shaped moldings form part of legs for the chairs.

42

Entrance hall showing Napoleon III chair and gilded console with green marble top. A timber Versailles pattern parquet floor was removed to reveal the original Venetian terrazzo floors within the palazzo, many of which were made with colored stone that are now rare and difficult to source.

"Our homes are the closest we come to creating an ideal and beautiful world for ourselves. An intimate space that is our very own, convenient and secure but above all a place that affords us comfort and joy."

Dining room, looking across the room through the existing antique mirrors. The demi lune console seen at a distance at the back of the mirror incorporates one of the fan coil units that are used to heat the room in winter and provide cooling in the summer.

The dining room. The theme of the ceiling painting is musical and the walls are decorated with trophies containing musical instruments; it is thought that this room may have originally served as a music room. The terrazzo floor with an elaborate patterned border was revealed once the parquet was removed. The current interior scheme probably originates mainly from the nineteenth century with some of the original decoration such as the ceiling painting surviving from an earlier period. Much of the east wall of the room appears to have been reconstructed possibly in the early part of the twentieth century, when the fireplace was removed. The flue was retained and was used for an oil burning stove also probably in the nineteenth century.

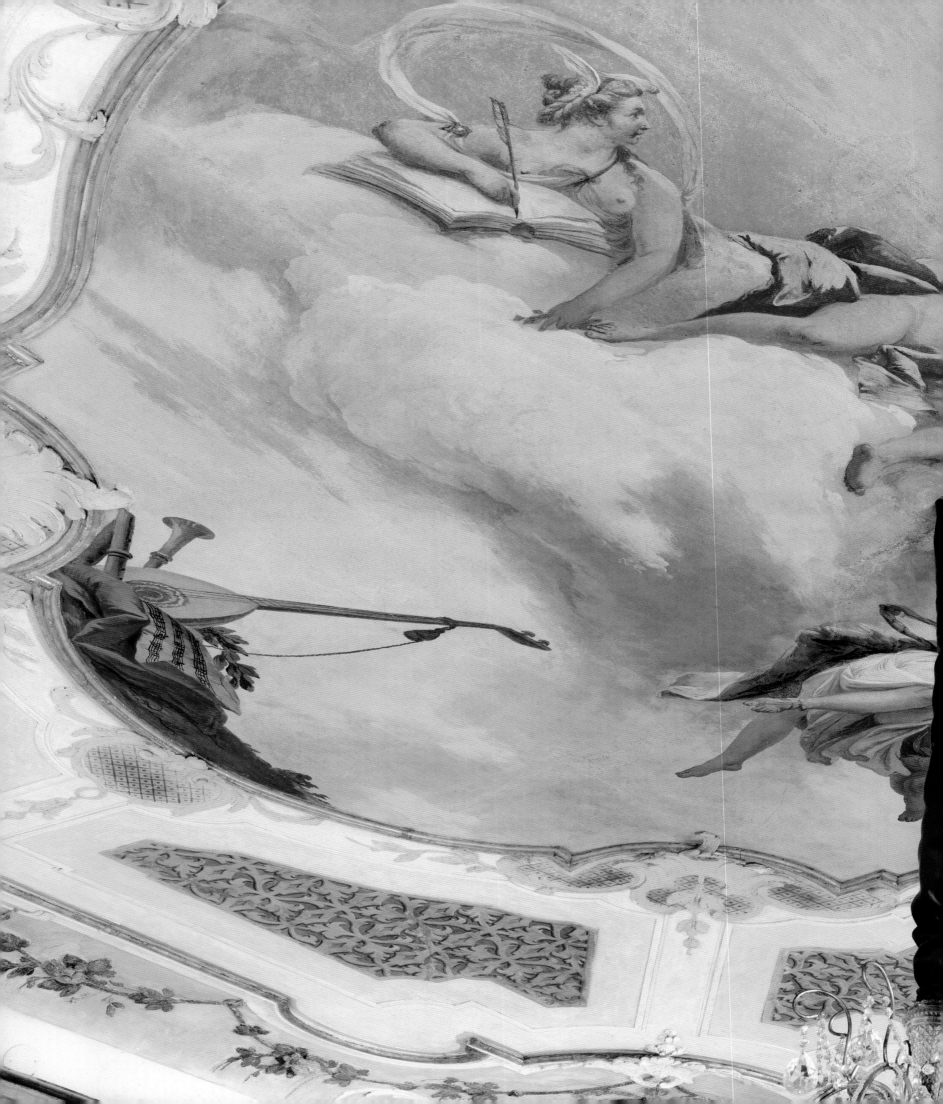

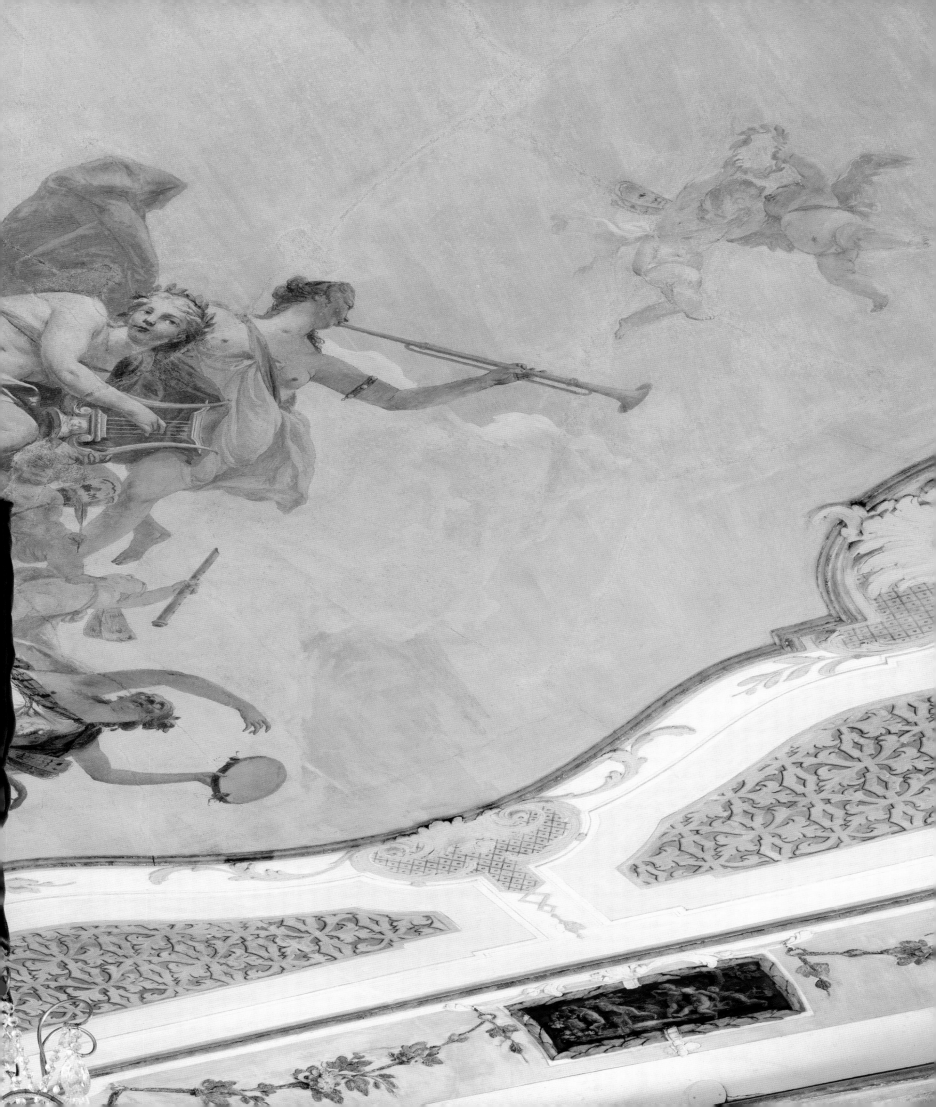

"This is where architecture and design play their part—providing connections to a sequence of rooms that through strategically placed openings, mirrors and devices such as screens and double doors, can be drawn together and opened up—to conjure, as if by magic, an impression of a large space in which we can welcome our guests with appropriate theater and ceremony."

(pages 48–49) The dining room ceiling painted by Cedini, who is thought to have been a pupil of Tiepolo in the eighteenth-century. The ceiling painting illustrates a musical scene showing Apollo with various nymphs and putti making music. The surrounding parts of the ceiling were probably embellished later in the nineteenth century.

(left) View looking through from the dining room into the main saloon. The panels above the doors are painted to match open fretwork that provides a view into the room from an upper mezzanine space. This could have been used as a musicians' gallery in the past but has been transformed into a small intimate library and study.

Entrance hall showing the elaborate gilded marble console table and chair. The chair is also from the Duchess of Roxburghe sale and was re-covered in specially designed fabric.

54

The breakfast room created beside the new kitchen below the mezzanine of the dining room. One of the reasons that it is thought that the palazzo may have been designed as a casino is that the mezzanine level provides a vantage point with views into the rooms below that would allow gambling to be discreetly supervised, an early form of CCTV you might say.

"Home is a sanctuary to which we retire to relax surrounded by all the things that make us happy and remind us of the places and people that we enjoy. It is a repository where we keep mementos of the events and achievements that define our lives and the objects to which, for one reason or another, we have become so intimately attached."

57

The Biedermeier Room is one of the entirely new rooms created by John Simpson within the palazzo. The trompe l'oeil transcenae panels and coffered ceiling as well as the borders used to embellish the walls use digital technology to create bespoke wallpaper patterns for the purpose. The large painting on the wall above the sofa is an oil on canvas by Antonia Simpson of her brother Nicholas.

58

View of Biedermeier Room showing the trompe l'oeil coffers on the ceiling created using bespoke, especially designed wallpaper. This would have been prohibitively expensive without the digital technology now available to print small, limited runs.

63

(pages 60–61) Detail of the wallpaper embellishment strips used in the Biedermeier Room. These are designed and printed to the correct lengths and applied directly to the walls. *(left)* The main bedroom showing the restored late nineteenth-century wall decoration. Three different schemes for the room were uncovered under various layers of paint. The original Venetian terrazzo floor was also uncovered beneath parquet flooring.

64

The main bedroom showing the four-poster bed which is an English Georgian design and came restored complete with silk hangings from a house in Tuscany. The large nineteenth-century painting on the wall behind depicts the Sibyl seated. The room is further embellished with oil paintings and prints and a specially commissioned new chandelier from Murano.

"A home arranged around a series of separate rooms will allow family members to enjoy different activities that would be incompatible otherwise in one open plan space, with one listening to or playing a musical instrument while another is quietly meditating or reading a book in another."

German ceramic switches based on a 1930s pattern were specified, providing appropriate fittings in keeping with the spirit of the palazzo. In order to operate you need to turn the switch so that you are literally turning the light on.

68

The Pompeiian Bedroom, created from space
previously occupied by the club's bar. The
arch above the bed was inserted and the ceiling
raised. New terrazzo was laid and digital
technology was used, as in the other rooms,
for the fabric for the bedcover and for
the embellishment of the walls.

(pages 70–71) The antechamber to the Pompeiian bedroom was created from what was the kitchen area serving the bar. The ceramic tiles on the walls and floor were removed, the walls covered with silk wallpaper and an oak timber floor laid. *(right)* The bathroom to the main bedroom was created out of small cabinet rooms, which may have originally been used for a similar purpose as bathing or dressing rooms. Plaster of different colors, called pasta embellishment, commonly used in Venice in the early part of the eighteenth century, has been employed for the wall decoration. The arch above the bath hides a nineteenth-century stair to the mezzanine area above that intrudes into the space. With the help of a high-level mirror, the missing section of decorated plaster ceiling taken out in the nineteenth century is suitably disguised.

The kitchen was created out of the space that was previously occupied by the gents and ladies loos. The kitchen uses robust commercially produced kitchen cabinets embellished with special polished oak handles and a cornice with a gray granite worktop and splash back.

II

BELSIZE PARK, LONDON

Each of the Simpsons' houses expresses an aspect of John's architectural personality—how could they not? But their residence at Belsize Park, which has been the main family home for thirty years, is particularly revealing of his imagination. There was a challenge when he bought the first flat around 1980: how to make two grand rooms for entertaining out of what had become a series of poorly divided spaces? As time went on, the other challenge came: how to incorporate the neighboring flats, as he and Erica were able to buy them, into a logical and harmonious whole, without impinging on rooms he had already created? Both called for ingenuity. John likens the process to doing a jigsaw puzzle in three dimensions. It is something at which he excels.

Belsize is supposed to derive from *bel assis* in old French, meaning beautifully sited. It was originally a farm on the slopes below Hampstead, based around the seventeenth-century Belsize House. After Belsize House had been demolished in 1853, the area around it was developed with large semidetached houses with generous porticos and much stucco. This was the neighborhood in which John had been living since the mid-1970s. As he walked down Belsize Park—which, despite its name, is a street—he formed the idea that the ground-floor rooms of the houses there would be ideal for entertaining. They were large, with high ceilings and generous window bays to the street. Eventually he noticed that a house had been shut off behind hoardings: a builder was converting what had previously been rented flats to properties for sale. Although it had yet to come onto the market, he and Erica succeeded in buying the ground floor.

Not only had the flat been poorly subdivided but all the Victorian details had been torn out. Neither of these apparent negatives was the obstacle it might sound. John had, in effect, a tabula rasa, on which he could work his own magic. This meant liberating the grand spaces at the front and back of the house, contriving to fit the working parts of the home into mysteriously invisible and previously unthought-of spaces, and designing every detail of the moldings and décor from scratch. It suited

him down to the ground. John is one of the few living architects who, in an ideal world, has complete control over domestic projects: furniture, curtains, fabrics, architectural fittings—all are drawn by him and made to his specifications. No world is more ideal than that of his own home.

Let us walk up the front steps. We enter a hallway, created—though you would not now know it—from space left over from the staircase leading to the flats on other floors. This entrance hall—really the outer of two—is dignified by an abbreviated cornice and a pair of tall arches, decorated with the sparest of moldings à la Soane. We do not linger long enough to register that the arches may not quite be an exact pair: one is wider than the other, but who notices as they are welcomed and proceed to the flat? The left-hand arch contains the staircase—or does not quite contain it, since the lowest steps spill out and curl around the jamb; it leads to flats above now owned by the Simpsons and tenanted. Set into the right-hand arch is a doorframe, giving into an inner hall that is vaulted, rusticated and has a black and white floor. Straight ahead of us, high up, is an antique bust. The entrance to the Simpson's quarters is on the right. But pause a moment before going in: the inner hall, although a small space, holds secrets. For the rustication conceals a hidden door to the kitchen, improving the circulation for parties (when John and Erica appear to be ubiquitous, popping up where least expected). Another concealed door gives onto what was originally a wine cellar, now used to store recycling bins. Surprise, spatial ingenuity, drama—these qualities are essentially Simpson and integral to all John and Erica's homes.

We go into the drawing room. This is a highly Classical and yet eclectic space, with memories of Rome, French Empire and the Vienna of the Biedermeier years combining to form a richly colored whole. The loss of the Victorian cornice, which would have been a fussy affair, has been made good by one of dentilated form, appropriate to the generally Neoclassical character of the furniture. Beneath it,

(above left) Klismos chairs and torchères designed by John Simpson for the Fellows' Dining Room at Gonville and Caius College, Cambridge. These chairs are deigned to stack and have robust cast aluminium rear legs, patinated to look like bronze. They are the only design for a Klismos chair known that is able to do this.
(above right) The tables, Klismos chairs and the torchères for Caius College were designed so that they can be combined to work as one long dining table that runs the whole length of the Fellows' Dining Room.

the walls have been painted Pompeiian red (John might have reserved it for the dining room but that room faces north, making a dark color infeasible). In sumptuous contrast, the upholstery of chairs and sofa is in a lemon-yellow silk, woven in France. These were the days before the technology existed to print to high standards on fabric: a "cheat" that John has since used to save on the exorbitant cost of woven silk and allow him to design his own patterns.) The voile of the curtain draperies is screen printed with an anthemion motif. The window bay is large enough to accommodate a grand piano.

The demi lune console for the dining room at the master's lodge at Gonville and Caius College, Cambridge, disguises a radiator behind the linen folds of the drum.

In the 1990s, John had an incentive to design the family's furniture: the market for antiques was—in that distant era—still strong and it was cheaper to have his own made. The same goes for the chimney piece, which is also a Simpson confection. A relatively plain marble surround is enlivened by flamboyant console brackets. Reader, would you guess it? Those console brackets are not, like the rest of the design, marble but plaster that has been marbled to match—and was of course far cheaper to produce. The black urns, seemingly black marble, are also painted wood. Some of the pieces in the room would have been unavailable at Christie's: for example, the John-designed torchères bearing glass shades were originally made for the Fellows' Combination Room at Gonville and Caius College in Cambridge. The herm heads on the mantelpiece are of the same origin, made by Stevensons of Norwich.

How, you ask, is it heated? Look at those pedestals, beneath the tripods that John conjured up for them. They conceal the radiators. Above, what appears to be a sconce disguises a burglar-alarm sensor. This is not the end of the room's wonders—to one of which we shall return later—but for now let's move, through a short-vaulted passage, to the dining room. Whereas the drawing room has a projecting bay, this is graced by a bow window. It is where the Christmas tree stands in December. At other than party times, the centerpiece of the room is a dining table, surrounded by John's take on the klismos chair of antiquity, richly veneered and inlaid. (The version made for Caius has a cast aluminum back that is stronger than wood.) The dining table is a sacred object: this is not a family

that likes to eat in the kitchen, and food, always of the best, is honored by ceremony. The walls, whose cornice is made of repeating anthemia, are painted Soane yellow.

Before John got at it, the kitchen occupied a space that had been ineptly carved from one of the big rooms. This did not suit John's vision at all. As a workaday room, it should be subservient to the architecture and tucked away where it could not be seen. He found a place for it next to the dining room: it is reached by a concealed door in the passage from the drawing room. (A matching concealed door, on the

other side of the passage, gives into a bathroom.) Above the kitchen, John contrived to fit a spare bedroom. Well, nobody would say there was much space to do this in—but John had an answer to that. The spare bed, built in, is reached by steps. Visitors who sleep in it are quite unaware that the piece of furniture beneath them is hollow; the void gives extra height to the kitchen. Similarly, don't try to open the central doors of one of the Biedermeier cabinets in the drawing room: they are false. Behind them are a dishwasher and work surface belonging to the kitchen. Space has been so cleverly stolen that nobody who was not in on the job would be aware of the theft. Not that the cabinets are a complete fraud from the drawing room's point of view: they also conceal loudspeakers and a heating duct.

That spare bedroom was designed in the manner of a ship's cabin: everything in its place and not an inch to spare. The window that you may have noticed behind the antique bust in the inner hall provides borrowed light. So does the one closed by crisscrossed transennae in the dining room, placed too high to see into.

In due course, the Simpsons' first child, Nicholas, was born and they had to surrender their own bedroom (the steps to the bed made the spare room impractical for an infant). It was time to expand. Fortunately, they got word that the ground floor of the next-door house was about to come onto the market, and they bought it. Openings were knocked through. In the new flat, the mid-nineteenth-century details had been preserved, which, although weaker in point of design, was felicitous. The corresponding space to the dining room became a library.

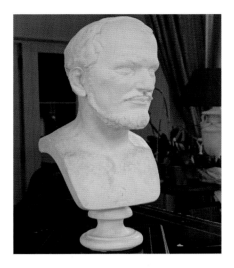

One advantage of the new flat was that it came with a garden. Sadly, it faces north, making it less than ideally suited to plants—but that only opens another opportunity for architecture. Columns made from bamboo canes give order. Other adjacent flats were bought as they came up, allowing the Simpsons' home to expand further; but they missed the chance to buy the basement flat beneath their first purchase. John has regretted it ever since. It would have enabled the gardens of the two houses to be made into one, with the possibility of making a more ambitious—and floriferous—scheme. It was not to be. That, however, merely opened yet another architectural prospect. The Simpsons needed a country house. They found it (or created it) at Harewell Hall.

This bust of John Simpson was sculpted by the Scottish sculptor Alexander Stoddart in 2002 for an exhibition by the artist called *Busts of Men*.

81

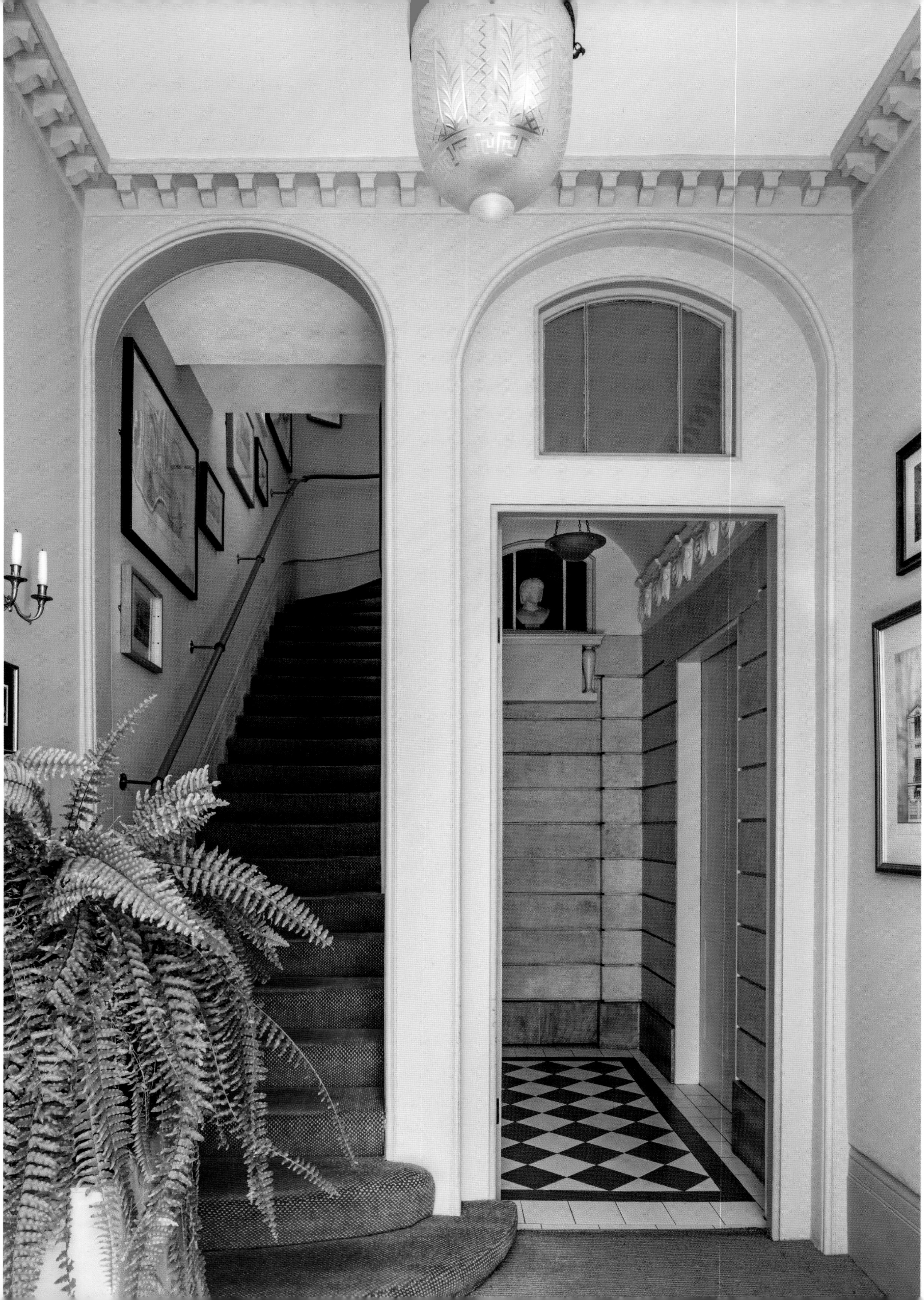

"Although it is often said that a person is judged by the company they keep, a brief visit to their home will reveal so much more about them; their interests and preferences, their values and aspirations as well their attitude and philosophy to life. This is why admitting someone into that inner sanctum of home will always be such a significant gesture of friendship and affection."

(page 82) The outer entrance hall at Belsize Park with two arches, one leading into the inner hall and the other accommodating a stair to the floors above.

(page 83) The inner entrance hall is rusticated to look like stone, which supports an archivolt embellished with bucrania (ox skulls) and roundels. The rustication disguises several jib doors to a cupboard under the stairs and to the kitchen. The internal window provides light to the kitchen.

(left) View looking into the mirror in the outer hall, showing the poster used to promote the Paternoster Square project in 1987, when John Simpson took on and overturned a modernist scheme next to St. Paul's Cathedral in London, with the support of the Prince of Wales.

86

The library at Belsize Park showing the half-size billiard table in the foreground and the Piranesi prints either side of the seventeenth-century capriccio above the sofa. The lamps are made from wood that has been painted to look like marble.

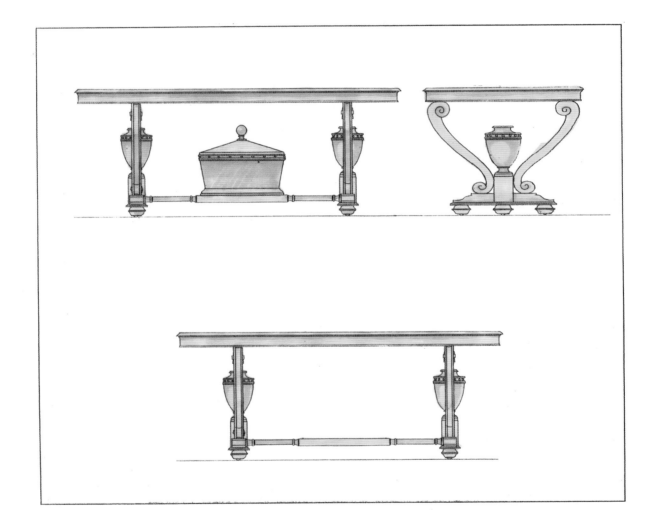

(pages 88–89) The library looking towards the balcony above the garden with obelisks either side. The fabric for the curtain is decorated with large Piranesi urns. The furniture in front of the window is all designed by John Simpson.

(left) Dining room. Ionic sideboard with supporting arches containing urns. This piece of furniture was originally designed as a reception desk for the office. Two Neoclassical candelabra together with a silver Warwick Vase with yellow tulips stand before a print of the Temple of Vesta, a wedding present from the architect Demetri Porphyrios. Drawings by John Simpson of a console table incorporating urns with an option for a champagne bath in the form of a sarcophagus below. A version of this was made with the lead lined sarcophagus for the Lord Colyton Room at Caius College in Cambridge.

(above) Drawings by John Simpson of a console table incorporating urns with an option for a champagne bath in the form of a sarcophagus below. A version of this was made with the lead-lined sarcophagus for the Lord Colyton Room at Caius College in Cambridge.

"The arrangement and physical nature of the house sets the criteria by which we live. It determines the ritual which, in all probability, is the single most predictable constant of our daily existence. It provides comfort during difficult times and the backdrop to which we bring up and educate our children."

(pages 92–93) The drawing room. The interior to this room is entirely new, the Victorian chimney piece and ceiling moldings having been removed before the Simpsons arrived. The small side tables, the torchères, the yellow chairs and the wall cabinet are designed by John Simpson. At either side of the chimney piece hang paintings by Carl Laubin. On the mantelpiece is a limewood model of the market building from Paternoster Square, surmounted by a maquette of a statue of Playfair erected in Glasgow by Alexander Stoddart. While the chimney piece is marble, the brackets to either side of it are wood, painted to blend in.

(left) All furniture serves a function. The pedestal below tripod standing behind the table to the left of the picture houses four flat steel radiators and provides the heating to the room. A hole at the top under the tripod lets warm air out which the bowl of the tripod disperses as it rises into the room.

(above) John Simpson's sketches for a side table and a torchère, both with tripod bases.

(right) Detail of the Madame Récamier chaise longue designed in blue for Ashfold House and in green for Belsize Park. The upholstery fabric is by Lelièvre, Paris.

(pages 98–99) Drawing room looking toward the bay window. The two sconces either side of the window incorporate PIR burglar detectors. *(right)* Drawing room looking towards the double doors that can be flung open to invite guests into the dining room. The left-hand side cabinet with the wooden sarcophagus is false: the interior is actually part of the kitchen and houses equipment that would have otherwise been impossible to accommodate in the small space. The segmental arches provide a housing for loudspeakers. The side table and yellow upholstered chair were designed and used at Ashfold House and at Belsize Park. The bronze torchères designed for the fellows' dining r oom at Caius College are patinated here in a dark color.

"Our houses need to be capable occasionally of transformation from small, cozy spaces that an intimate group might enjoy, to a suitable venue for a birthday or Christmas party. This is where the architecture and design play their part, providing connections to a sequence of rooms through strategically placed openings, mirrors and devices such as screens and double doors."

Pearwood model of the Market Hall Building at Paternoster Square in the City of London together with candlestick and wine on the sideboard.

From the curved bay, a Roman statue of
a Vestal Virgin watches over the dining table;
she holds a model of the Temple of Vesta.
The bases for the tripods house radiators and
the sconces either side of the window conceal
PIR burglar alarm detectors. The torchères are
used in the dining room, as designed for Caius
College Cambridge, with the bronze patinated
in green.

Dining room looking toward the study. The
walls were painted in a yellow similar to that
used in the drawing room at the Soane Museum
in Lincoln's Inn Fields in order to brighten up
a north facing room. John Soane used to refer
to this color as Turner Yellow in deference
to the painter who was a friend and a fellow
academician at Burlington House.

"Inevitably the organization and form of a house are not there simply to provide shelter and security but to facilitate a lifestyle that we have chosen for ourselves and for those around us. The location of a dining room at the center of a house for instance will inevitably determine how often a family will share a meal around a table rather than just snack in the kitchen or eat individually while watching television."

The kitchen, showing cabinets built in European oak with gray granite worktops. The cabinets feature three-quarter engaged
Doric pilasters and corbel brackets with a cornice at ceiling level. The mouse holes in the base at floor level ventilate the refrigerator behind.

"One of the joys of working on my own houses is that I have the time to be more than usually thoughtful and disciplined and yet at the same time philosophical, playful and even whimsical."

Looking into the study, showing cupboards either side of the day bed. The inner surfaces of the cupboards facing the bed are flat panel radiators with convector heaters in the housings above. An oil painting by Carl Laubin of the Defence and National Rehabilitation Centre designed by John Simpson hangs above the daybed. The light fitting on the ceiling was designed originally for Buckingham Palace.

III

HAREWELL HALL, WHERWELL, HAMPSHIRE

When the Simpsons' two sons, Nicholas and Alexander, were at Winchester College, the family needed a base in Hampshire, where the boys could unwind during the relative short period they were allowed out of school. They found a cottage in the pretty, thatched village of Wherwell; carbon dating revealed that the timbers had been cut in 1495. Alas, a fire caused by a neighbor's chimney set their own dwelling alight. This, however, was only a spur to more architecture. Not only was the cottage, in time, restored but John saw possibilities in the land that they owned next door. What followed would be a triumph both of homemaking and navigating the planning system. A substantial new house arose where nobody had imagined it would be possible.

The site lies in a crucial part of the village, next to the church. This gave it particular sensitivity in planning terms. John faced the problem squarely, by consulting his neighbors. What would be necessary for them to tolerate a new building in their midst? The answer came back, thatch. It was important that any new structure should be roofed in the way of the rest of the street. For a Classical architect, thatch is not an obvious material but then John is not only a Classicist but a portent of the tradition which has been such a distinctive part of English visual culture: the Picturesque. Buildings captivate through the stories they tell. This is obvious in the case of an old structure. The English way is to keep a good part of the existing work, so that any new work is enriched by its contrast with, or continuation of, the old. It can also apply to new projects. In the 1980s, John designed a new settlement at Donnington Grove in Berkshire which—radically for the time—would have given the appearance of being an organic growth, immemorial in the center with villas of 1820, as it might seem, around the outside. Sadly this, being outside the area allocated for development by the local authority, did not leave the drawing board. But the principle remained valid. It emerges again at Harewell Hall, as the Simpsons have called the new house, built where perhaps only John could have succeeded in raising it.

Harewell Hall, with the Italian garden on the south, showing the conservatory with pergolas either side. The chimney rises between the main half-timbered building and the masonry kitchen extension to the east. In former times, it would have been common for additions, particularly kitchens and chimney stacks that were added to houses of this kind, to be built of masonry, as brick became more affordable as a construction material.

1. View looking across Upper Donnington from Flats on the high ground.

There was an important Benedictine nunnery at Wherwell before the Dissolution of the Monasteries. Founded in the tenth century, it was destroyed by fire, then refounded in 1227, when the abbess diverted a stream from the river Test under the abbey. A thirteenth-century barn still exists. The cottage was part of an outlying building that stood on the site of Harewell Hall. The fact that most of it was demolished centuries ago does not alter its validity to planners. Where the footprint of a previous building exists, another of the same size can be erected—and John could argue that, however big, the result was only an extension to the existing cottage. Being medieval, the vanished structure would almost certainly have been a hall house, and this gave John the first clue to his design. He does not usually build in green oak but here was an opportunity to do so. There would be a double-height room, going up to open rafters in the medieval fashion, with a thatched roof above. Crowning all would be a lantern: an essential feature of medieval halls, originally needed to let out the smoke from the central hearth and later kept out of a sense of familiarity and status. Wooden rooms have good acoustics and the hall at Harewell is no exception. There is a grand piano here, as at Belsize Park and the Palazzo Grimani. Foremost among the family musicians is Alexander, training to be an opera singer. The room is perfect for informal concerts. A broad staircase of shallow tread gives off what would have been the "high" (or lord's) end of the hall, of easy ascent because we all get old in time. This does not ape the type or position of medieval stairs but Harewell is a caprice, not a pastiche.

As well as a lantern, a hall invariably had a screens passage, crossing from one side to the other and another means of ventilating the room. John imagined that his might have been placed in the age of Wren, with arched doorcase and columns. There is a minstrel's gallery above. Beyond the screen, the main stairs come into view—and beyond them is a drawing room, added, we are invited to imagine, in the Regency. At the far end, the broad French windows are swagged with curtains, in what friends have come to recognize as the Simpson manner. As in Venice, the furniture—call it

Sketch of Upper Donnington, showing the picturesque formation of the buildings as seen from the high ground.

114

antique Roman, call it Biedermeier—is upholstered in a wholly twenty-first-century fabric, digitally printed to imitate woven silk (at a fraction the cost).

The view beyond is inviting. What is to be considered as garden building, what as house, in planning terms? Who can say? But certainly there is a garden room and then what the eighteenth century would have called a canal; the twenty-first century knows it as a swimming pool, with an articulated roof like a lobster's shell which slides over in times of bad weather. The canal is flanked to either side by rose arbors, alternately red and white, in false perspective. At the end, to commemorate a tree that fell, stands a maypole with ropes descending; eventually the ropes will be entwined with creepers. The waterspout from which the canal is fed takes the form of a dolphin, as an allusion to the mythical cockatrice associated with Wherwell Abbey: one was said to have swum up the watercourse under the abbey and made away with certain nuns who had disappeared (a more prosaic explanation is that they had run away). The dolphin was made at half-scale in Alexander Stoddart's studio, then scanned and carved using a CNC machine; the hollow interior contains the plumbing.

A porch has been made from primitive columns—very primitive, indeed, because the columns are formed from no more than bundles of bamboo canes, banded together. This is a playful allusion to the theory that Classical architecture developed from wooden construction, explained by Vitruvius in his description of a primordial dwelling or primitive hut. It is an idea that Simpson explored in the Pipistrelle Pavilion built by students of the Prince of Wales's Institute of Architecture at Barnes. This combined the rationalism of Soane, who inquired into the first principles of architecture in his Royal Academy lectures, with the Arts and Crafts tradition important to Prince Charles. At Harewell, the porch simply adds to the charm.

115

(pages 116–17) Harewell Hall's design is based on a house that once existed on an adjacent site in the village built in 1495. It is a half-timbered house, twenty-two meters long, with an oak frame and a thatched roof.

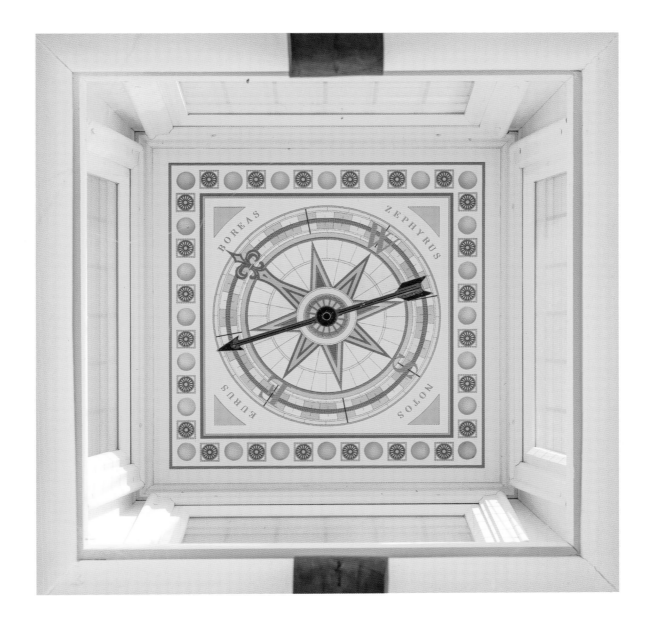

(pages 118–19) The entrance elevation, showing the large oriel window and lantern that light the interior of the hall and the main entrance door that leads through to a screens passage inside.

(left) The lantern, a familiar feature of medieval and Tudor country houses. Historically, lanterns replaced vents that originally provided an outlet for smoke from a brazier used for heating inside the hall. This lantern is designed to incorporate louvers and provides ventilation to the hall, operated if required by two pull cords within the hall. The glazing in the lantern is in amber glass so as to give the impression that the sun always shines at Harewell.

(above) Looking up into the lantern from the hall. An arrow is connected to the weathervane outside, so that you can check on the direction of the wind before leaving the house.

(pages 122–23) These details show some of the embellishment: the coat of arms above the entrance and the stained-glass embellishment in the oriel window. The coat of arms was modelled digitally and carved and carved by a tool called a CNC machine connected to a computer.

(right) Halewell Hall, in Hampshire, and the swimming pool. The water appears to run through a water gate underneath the building. This is a reference to the canal that was constructed to divert water from the river Test to provide running water in the kitchens at the nearby Wherwell Abbey. Local legend has it that a cockatrice would swim into the abbey using the route so as to abduct nuns. In practice, the water gate provides convenient access to the swimming pool from the conservatory inside the house.

(left) The Classical vinery in the kitchen garden is built using rustic Doric columns made from bundles of bamboo. The cottages behind are the surviving elements of the 1495 building that inspired the design of Harewell Hall.

(pages 128–29) The rustic Doric pergola by the conservatory is a pleasant place to sit at the south-western corner of the house. Together with the vinery, it frames the entrance drive and is a reminder of the rustic origins of the Doric order in Classical architecture.

(pages 130–31) The Fig Loggia forms one side of a small courtyard on the east side of the screens passage. The courtyard and loggia provide another sunny and sheltered location in which to sit. The loggia is also used to grow figs under a glass roof and provides a backdrop to the view you get as you look along the screens passage when entering the house.

(above) Herm head originally designed for the Fellows' Dining Room at Gonville and Caius College in Cambridge. Two of his brothers can be seen on the mantlepiece of the drawing room at 50 Belsize Park.

One of the archways supporting roses that flank the Italian garden on the south side of the house. They are planted with alternate red and white climbing roses. This one supports the highly scented Tess of the d'Urbervilles red roses.

136

(pages 134–35) The Italian garden from the
conservatory. It is laid out in false perspective
to exaggerate the length of the garden with the
Italian cypress trees and the rose arches getting
smaller as they recede into the distance. The vista
is terminated by a curved bench with a pergola
centered around a pole with ropes supporting a
canopy of climbing roses above. The arrangement
is a reference to Karl Friedrich Schinkel at
Charlottenhoff in Postsdam.

(right) View from inside the tented conservatory
showing the entrance into the pool. The triple-sash
windows are designed to slide up into one another
so as to provide enough height for people to walk
out into the garden either side.

"Home is the backdrop and stage to display the objects and artifacts that I have collected and a place where I can enjoy the company of friends."

(pages 138–39) Looking from the drawing room into the conservatory. The furniture is a version of that designed for Palazzo Grimani in Venice. This suite is made from light-colored beechwood with a green printed fabric to contrast with the Pompeiian red of the walls. The mantelpiece is in white marble with console brackets based on those from the entrance doorcases to the Erechtheion on the Acropolis in Athens.

(left) A collection of busts, cameos, urns and oil lamps surmounted by a screen built of architectural building blocks either side of a black urn in the library.

(pages 142–43) The library, is a very light and sunny room at the northwest corner of the house. A white plaster model of a domed circular Doric temple sits on the library table.

(left) The kitchen is designed around a large oak table with a dark gray granite top in the center of the room. The tabletop is at worktop height so that it can be used standing up or sitting on a bar stool. The space under the table is used to provide additional storage with drawers for cutlery and spices on one side and containers for collecting recycling waste on the other.

"Home is also the name we give to the place that we grow up in or where we raise a family. It reflects our roots, the world that belongs to us, the values that we identify with that set us apart from those around us. It defines our cultural and aesthetic preferences, the lifestyle we are accustomed to and the habits that have become the ritual of our daily lives."

The main hall at the center of the house with its green oak hammer beam roof, which was built in the traditional manner using using pegged motice and tenon joints. A large arched mirror behind the table is crowned with a series of Palladian ball finials and provides a reflected view of the screens passage and the gallery from the entrance. A second staircase through an opening on the right of the mirror leads up to the master bedroom suite whilst the one on the left leads to the library. Light streams into the hall from the west facing oriel for most of the day. In the oriel, on a column pedestal stands a copy of the a bust of Achilles by William Theed, made in 1856 for the gallery above the Grand Staircase at Buckingham Palace. This pedestal is the upper part of the Ionic order from the temple of Apollo Epicurius at Bassae used by John Simpson in his design for the Fellows' dining room at Gonville and Caius College in Cambridge.

(left) Dining table in hall. The timber staircase and Classical screen supporting the gallery above were made in European oak from France by Applewood Joinery in Hampshire, who were also responsible for the shallow Gothic arch behind. The contrast between the two hints that the screens passage might be a latter addition to the interior.

(above) Contemplative nook in the minstrel's gallery above the hall.

IV

ASHFOLD HOUSE, EAST SUSSEX

Ashfold House in East Sussex was the ideal country house for the time it was designed, in 1984. Domestic ambitions have expanded since then but in that time of crisis and uncertainty, with Mrs. Thatcher in power but confidence still at a low ebb, most people wanted a compact, livable house that would not be too expensive to heat. As country houses go, Ashfold is small, but John has filled it to the rafters with architecture. South-facing, it stands within the kitchen garden of a previous country house, and is therefore sheltered; with the benefit of an octagonal Victorian dairy to serve as a guest apartment. Services do not obtrude to spoil the beauty of the proportions. Wall sconces bearing candles incorporate the infrared sensors of the security system. Thermostats, electricity sockets and other banalities have been hidden in the architecture, which is Classical, in the manner of Sir John Soane. The moldings are pared down, often incised; externally the sash windows are punched into the brick walls without surrounds.

View of Ashfold House, looking through an archway in the existing brick serpentine wall built by Lord Nelson's sister when she lived at Ashfold in the late eighteenth-century.

151

This was John Simpson's first major building, designed for his parents at the start of his practice. There was time to think about every detail (there is always time for this purpose in John's practice). The plan not only provides a series of convenient rooms but also drama. It is square, like Palladio's Villa Rotonda and Lord Burlington's Chiswick House; but unlike those party buildings, built for show and not intended to be slept in overnight, the facades are not the same. The model is Soane's own country house, Pitzhanger Manor at Ealing, which Soane developed from an existing house by his mentor, George Dance. Both are exercises in pure form, where the discipline of the volume serves to stimulate invention; the Picturesque comes to the rescue of architects needing to accommodate the requirements of a functioning home within the self-imposed constraints. There is, however, also a pure cube at Ashfold: it is to be found in the conservatory, reached by a short passage.

At Ashfold's center is a hall that goes up the full height of the house. To give more space to the drawing room, it projects three feet out into a rectangular bay, which is carried up onto the floor above (where it gives room for a study). Soane does the same

thing at his house in Lincoln's Inn Fields. There are some ways, though, in which a modern house can go one better than Soane. Central heating means that it is not necessary to box off the main staircase or incorporate lobbies as buffer zones against draughts. The absence of servants' rooms makes the plan more compact.

On each of the four sides of the hall is an arch, one of which frames the stair. It is made of wood but painted and detailed like stone—a piece of trompe l'oeil that John learned from the eighteenth-century architect Sir Robert Taylor, an early exponent of the villa. Narrow doors hidden in the side reveals lead to a bathroom and the kitchen, but they remain entirely inconspicuous when closed. Immediately behind the stair shelters the breakfast room, which seems to have been created out of practically nothing, its depths being little more than that of a bow window. The bow continues onto the first floor to light the stair. The result is a piece of spatial complexity not always found in modern Classicism of a more Palladian bent.

West elevation of Ashfold House, showing the conservatory in the foreground with the main block of the house behind. A rooflight beneath the ball finial lights a double-height tribune over the entrance hall at the center of the house. A terrace outside with steps into the garden faces south.

The scale helped stimulate invention. John says that "smallness of scale tends to concentrate the mind to some extent. On a big building, there would have been less justification for playing the kind of tricks we did at Ashfold." One of the best effects is achieved in the upper story of the hall. Each side of the gallery is fronted by a sarcophagus and urns. The view across the void and out into the landscape is a *coup de theatre*, all the better for being unexpected in a building of this size.

Downstairs the drawing room runs the full length of the south front. It is a very light room, having windows on three sides. The three windows on the garden front, repeating the arch motif that recurs throughout the house, open up onto the terrace. Floor-length windows are, John explains, another Regency feature which modern heating makes more practical. Here and elsewhere the shutters are typically ingenious: they hinge differently from conventional shutters, allowing them to fold back into boxes and be flush with the wall. This removes the need for deep window reveals. The mystery of how the shutters can close over the curtains is explained when one

152

discovers that the lower parts of the curtains are attached to them and also move. Internal shutters were preferred to double glazing to preserve the fineness of the detail. Shallow ceiling moldings divide the room into three.

The tripartite arrangement is echoed in the placing of the furniture, with a sofa and chaise longue facing each other across a rug. These are among many specially designed pieces: John's practice was designing furniture and draperies from earliest days. The chaise is consciously derived from those seen in Roman frescoes. Comfortable armchairs were also a requirement. The only chimney piece can be seen in the living room (designed as a dining room), with opulently curling consoles that contrast with the simple bead moldings elsewhere. John also designed the cabinets above the cupboards to either side, which contain video and television equipment. "Opening the doors onto the television makes viewing more of an event," says John. Nothing lacks an explanation in this most considered and rational of houses.

Section through Ashfold House, showing the roof-lit double-height tribune at the center of the house. The breakfast room can be seen under the half-landing of the main stair within the bay window facing east. The conservatory is an attached independent structure sitting in the garden to the west side of the house.

153

(pages 154–55) Front view. The north elevation of Ashfold House is based on a triumphal arch using brick with stucco and reconstructed stone dressings under a Welsh slate roof. The architecture of radical Classicism—rethinking the elements from first principles—recalls that of Sir John Soane in the Regency period. The gold finial on the roof incorporates a television aerial within.

159

(pages 156–57) South facade and terrace. The bay provides additional space required for the main drawing room across the south of the building and for the study/library space upstairs.

(left) A two-story bay on the east side of the building provides space for the stair landing with a breakfast room below. The breakfast room looks out onto a small garden with fig trees. The result is strongly volumetric.

"Despite putting such store by our privacy, we are nevertheless social beings. We are never happy to be in complete isolation and a home that has an outlook with views over its surroundings is highly prized and particularly so when combined with a garden or even just a simple balcony or small outside terrace."

The bay at night showing the interior of the breakfast room and the table that was designed for the space with the door behind leading to the cellar below.

The detailing of the brackets and the architrave to the half-landing, as well as the door to the cellar, derive from Egyptian precedents.

(left) The Ionic doorcase within the entrance door archway of the north facade frames a vista that runs right

through the house, culminating in a view looking out over the parkland on the south side of the house.

(above) Sketches by John Simpson for dining chairs and a round table supported on three brackets arranged around a central urn.

164

(above) The double-height top-lit tribune that runs the full height of the house and provides
views from the upper floor into the entrance hall and of the staircase below
(right) Looking across the upper part of the tribune into the study with a view over parkland on the south side of the house. The shutters either
side of the window to the study when closed reveal a series of paneled mirrors so the shutters can be closed in the evenings to reduce heat loss.

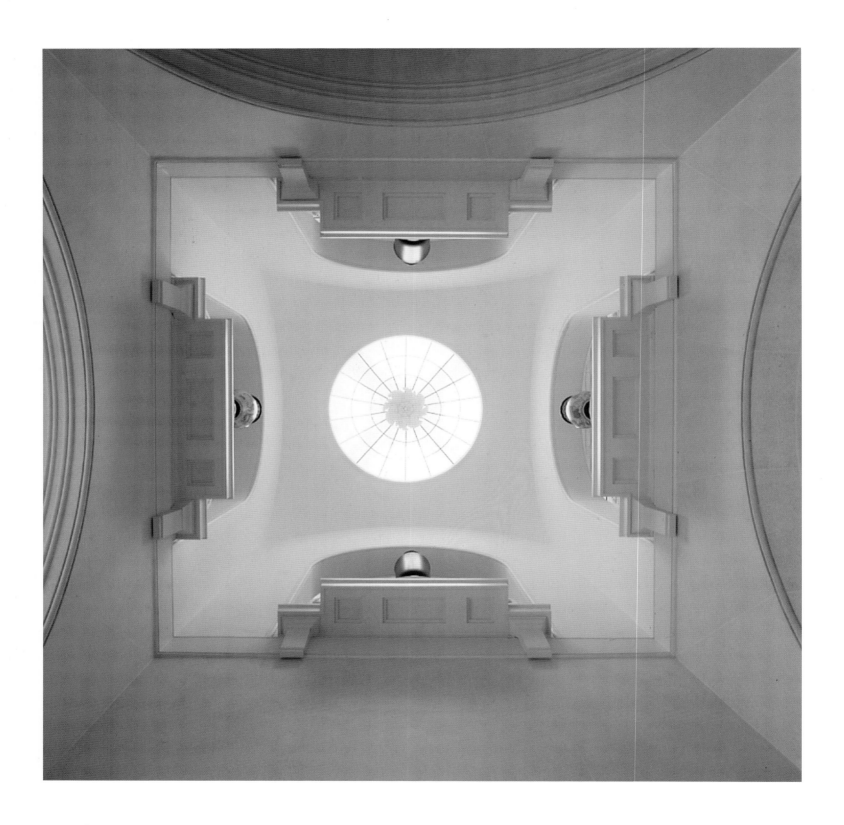

Looking up to the dome of the tribune. The design of the bookcases, symmetrically placed on all four sides, recalls Michelangelo and his work at the Medici Chapel in Florence. A glazed oculus to the dome illuminates the gallery that forms a library on the upper level and the hall below.

Looking along the stair from the library on the upper level of the tribune into the bay over the breakfast room. The balustrade of the half-landing is adorned with two tripods and an urn. The view through the upper clerestory window to the bay looks our over the rose garden to the east and beyond the serpentine wall built by Lord Nelson's sister when she lived at Ashfold.

(left) The vista that runs through the vaulted entrance hallway and the lower half of the tribune leads you through into the main drawing room and onto an outside terrace that overlooks the parkland.

(above) The layout of the rooms makes most of the surrounding parkland affording vistas across one room through to the next to reveal the view from a window into the gardens beyond.

The main drawing room runs the full width
of the south facade of the house. Cupboard
doors built into recesses in the wall open to
reveal shutters that run across the windows.
The shutters to the windows on the end walls
are mirrored so that they do not look oppressive
if they are shut during the day. A central French
window opens out onto the terrace. The plaster
embellishment on the ceiling is organized in
a tripartite design using Greek key incised
patterns arranged around recessed panels with
ball bead moldings.

The floor to the drawing room is oak parquet with an inlaid walnut pattern. The furniture including the Klismos chair, the chaise longue, the red chair and the tripod side table were all especially designed for Ashfold.

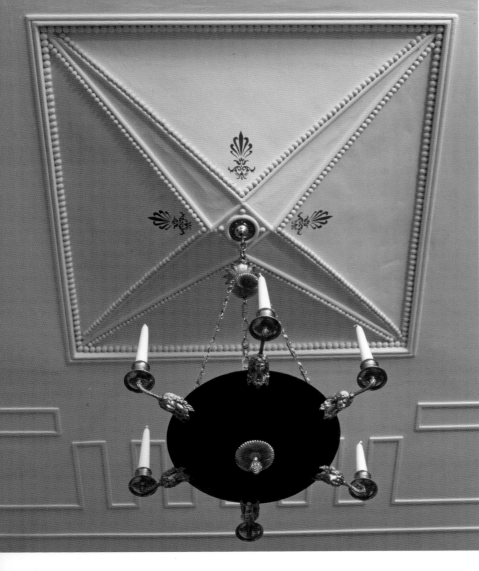

(above) Ceiling detail with light fitting in the sitting room.

(right) Klismos chairs with black horsehair upholstery together with
the beech round table were designed for the breakfast room. The cornice to
the half landing to the stair is supported by what appear to be the ends of
circular pole beams arranged in groups of three. The cornice above supports
a Kylix set within a shallow arch with a tripod either side. A roof light
with transenae in the vaulted ceiling to the stair hall provides
light from above.

(above) The furniture in the drawing room was designed for Ashfold House. The chaise longue is veneered with satinwood and unholstered with fabric by Lelièvre.

(right) Welsh dresser in the kitchen built in European oak. A worktop opens out in the form of a drawer to provide additional workspace during parties.

The sitting room incorporates built in cabinets either side of the chimney piece. The doors to the upper cabinet to the right reveals a television within while the lower cabinet to the left incorporates a turntable and a collection of vinyl long playing records. The arches under the upper cabinets are housings for speakers. The fire surround is made of Carrara marble with a cast iron fire back.

The sitting room furniture was specially designed for the room and upholstered with Lelievre silk fabric from Paris to match the curtains. At the time, the high cost of antiques made it cost-effective to have new pieces made; the market has changed since then but digital technology has made it cheaper to create striking fabrics. The ceiling like that in the drawing room uses incised Greek key patterns but this time arranged around a central plaster pendant supporting a regency light fitting. The cornice is the same as that in the drawing room except that the balls are arranged in repeating groups of three.

The conservatory is designed to give the impression of being in a garden pavilion outside the house. It has triple sash windows that open to provide two meter headroom so that you can walk out into the garden without hitting your head. The floor is in Carrara marble.

(above) Looking out from the breakfast room, you see the Old Model Dairy, built in the 1880s. The curved sash windows slide up into a pocket in the wall above so that they open high enough for people to walk out without hitting their head. The little panels between the windows open out to reveal a concertina style shutter that draws across the windows for security as well as thermal insulation.

(right) A glimpse into the kitchen from the breakfast room area showing the Italian checkerboard pattern for the floor. The kitchen cabinets are made from oak with solid gray granite worktops. Note the specially designed circular brass fitting you see in the foreground uses a traditional toggle swtich for the lights. Vertical shutters rise up in front of the kitchen windows from behind the cabinets, operated by counter balancing sash weights.

The interior of the dairy is marble lined and designed to keep the dairy produce cool and fresh through the warm summer months. It also has a painted pale blue plaster octagonal dome with panels at cornice level depicting the names of the principal milk producing cows on the estate. Roman tiles are used on the roof with cast iron columns supporting an overhanging eaves. Legend has it that craftsmen from northern Italy were brought to Sussex to build the dairy.

V

29 GREAT JAMES STREET, BLOOMSBURY

Great James Street is one of Bloomsbury's finest streets. On either side is a terrace of early eighteenth-century town houses, now offices, but little altered, except for occasionally lost glazing bars; facades of tawny stock brick with red facings are complemented by tall doorcases with fanlights and carved wooden hoods. It is London as it should be. Outside number 29 are a brass plate bearing words John Simpson Architects Limited and an entry phone that rarely seems to open the door so much as summon a person to open it (if only more did the same).

The reception desk in the Great James Street office incorporates a cast of part of the frieze from the Temple of Apollo Epicurius at Bassae. This was used to test various colors when a cast of the Frieze was commissioned from the British Museum for installation in the new Fellows' Dining Room at Gonville and Caius College.

You are not long in doubt as to the nature of the practice that is pursued here. The center of the downstairs waiting room is filled by a large architectural model of Paternoster Square, the cause célèbre of the 1980s when John, backed by the Prince of Wales, helped to defeat a monolithic modernist scheme next to St. Paul's Cathedral. The model is covered by a case of glass in ebonized wood, of the sort normally found in the museums of old-fashioned antiquarian societies who have not thrown out their nineteenth-century furniture. You wait on a sofa of John's design, whose Regency stripe has faded from its place in the window. Opposite is the reception desk, concealed behind a cast of a section of frieze from the Temple of Apollo Epicurius at Bassae, now in the British Museum. The Neoclassical architect C. R. Cockerell excavated the temple in the 1810s and the cast was commissioned from the museum for John's scheme at Gonville and Caius College, Cambridge: Cockerell designed the building that is now its library.

There are casts and models everywhere in this office, souvenirs of forty years of commissions. Behind the sofa, is a grand ceiling rose from the lecture hall of the Queen's Gallery at Buckingham Palace. In the fireplace, part of a Doric column, inspired by the austere order used at Bassae but more elaborate in decoration. It is another memory of Caius, as are the two lions on the mantelpiece, taken from a James II coat of arms that was copied for the hall. On the wall, a model of the new village proposed for Donnington in Berkshire in the 1980s, which would have got planning permission if only Nicholas Ridley had not resigned—he had been on the point of signing the relevant

paperwork when drummed from office. It was the first Poundbury-like scheme before Poundbury. "Models," John says, "are always a problem—you never know what to do with them after a project is finished. Clients find them too big to keep." Some, like the Donnington model, are hung vertically to save space. Around them are bird's-eye views, perspectives, elevations. It is like the trophy room of a big-game hunter, only the moose heads and tiger skins have been replaced by representations of buildings.

188

Two pedestals support more models, one of them for an architectural chess set whose pieces line up to form street facades. If that isn't ingenious enough for you, look beneath the cloth covering the pedestals: they are cabinets to hold files and toolboxes. An urn on a draped pedestal in the corridor conceals a fire sensor and fire extinguisher. This is a place of make-believe and metamorphosis. The ugliness of the twenty-first century comes in at the front door. Behold, in the twinkling of an eye, it has been hidden beneath Classical dress.

Come up the early-Georgian staircase, admiring the barley sugar twists of the balusters, three to a tread as you go. John's own office is on the first floor. There he is, at a long table heaped with drawings, with only a computer screen to remind us that this is 2020, not 1820, when the Prince Regent became George IV. There are genuine Regency touches to the room. When the original year leases fell in at the end of the eighteenth century, the detail of the paneled room was updated. This meant removing the box cornice, lowering the doors and chimney pieces, and reducing the moldings to door and window to a minimum. At some point, the Georgian glazing bars were removed from the windows: John has added anthemions to give interest, in what he describes as an Alexander "Greek" Thomson touch. Behind the paneling is a void that has proved an excellent place to hide service pipes and cabling.

This is another room full of samples and treasures. A section of relief sculpture shows Odysseus appealing for the protection of Queen Arete, part of Alexander Stoddart's frieze in the entrance hall of the Queen's Gallery. The plaster capital over the fireplace is from

a suite of Classical elements that John was commissioned to design, with the idea that they would be sold commercially; that customers could use the different parts to assemble their own Classical buildings, but only the capital survives as one of the prototypes. Above it is the anthemion of the Palladio Award, given for the Carhart Building on New York's East Ninety-Fifth Street, which has been described as the first fully Classical building to be erected for half a century. It stands beside a wooden mallet awarded by the Worshipful Company of Masons for the stonework of the Queen's Gallery. Another member of the Queen's Gallery are samples of scagliola (for columns) and bronze balustrade (for the staircase).

Model for the new development at Paternoster Square near St Paul's Cathedral in the City of London. This project was initially carried out to show how a traditional approach to designing cities would not only be more commercially viable but result in developments with a more beautiful and appropriate streetscape. Supported by the Prince of Wales, the development was taken up by leading developers Greycoat and Park Tower and is now accepted as the right approach to any city center development.

Here is the engine room of the office, where John's pencil initiates and corrects the designs. But architecture is also about construction, which involves meetings—and the number of people needed to be accommodated at them gets larger all the time. Fortunately, 29 Great James Street has a yard, big enough for a large, well-insulated shed. As a temporary structure, it could be installed without planning permission, thereby saving time at a moment when the office's workload had rapidly expanded. A workaday building need not betray its mass-produced origins. Externally the short passage beside the basement area by which the shed is reached is articulated by rustication and herms. The shed itself has been given a pediment and sash window. A similar transformation has been achieved inside it. Lo, here is a tent room, hung with yard upon yard of swagged ticking. Here is the true Simpson touch: an economical solution transported to another realm on the flying carpet of taste.

(left) Plaque at entrance of 29 Great James Street.

(above) Great James Street, off Theobalds Road in central London, was developed for J. Metcalfe in the 1720s. John Simpson Architects acquired the building in 1990 and the practice has been based there ever since.

(pages 192–93) The paneled interior to the offices at first floor level painted in Turner Yellow with Klismos chairs and table designed by the practice. A painting by Carl Laubin of Paternoster Square hangs above the mantelpiece. Part of the frieze commissioned for H. M. the Queen's Jubilee by Alexander Stoddart lies propped up against the wall with various models and plaster casts of moldings. The light fittings are those designed for the Queen's Gallery at Buckingham Palace.

(left) The reception space at ground floor. With space at a premium, models are hung on walls and column capitals placed on the hearth in the fireplace. A well-used version of the Mme. Récamier chaise longue provides somewhere for visitors to sit and appreciate the models and plaster casts on display.

(above) In the hallway at the entrance is a fire extinguisher stand. Placed on an Ionic column base, it appears as a column draped with a red cloth embellished with anthemions supporting an urn. The base of the urn contains the firebreak button on the front and the siren on the back.

(near right) The Klismos chairs used in the conference room were originally designed as stacking chairs for the Fellows' Dining Room at Gonville and Caius College.

(far right) Chessmen designed as terraced houses with pediments, pavilions and triumphal arches with pawns forming a covered loggia. The set can be used to create different urban configurations of picturesque streets and squares. Designed by John Simpson in the 1980s.

"We all want to feel we belong and connected to the things around us and especially so to the natural world which is so often vital to our sense of wellbeing, health and sanity. That is why a home where the level of sunlight inside can keep us aware of the time of day and the weather outside can be so much more satisfying as a place to live."

The staircase at 29 Great James Street with barley sugar twist balusters original to the building. Unusually, for such an ornate pattern, this staircase is in softwood and has been scumbled in the eighteenth-century manner. The staircase walls hang as a gallery displaying the work of the practice. The conference room extension built into the yard at the back can be seen through the window.

(above) Herms are used to create a link between the historic building and the conference room extension at the rear. The structure is made of timber and painted to look like stucco.

(right) View of the rear extension in the garden with its pedimented front that was built over the vaulted scullery and storage spaces in the basement below.

"For an architect, designing your own home is an opportunity to explore ideas that you have been itching to try out and do so without the necessity of convincing a client of their merit or having to find ways to weave them into a strictly controlled budget. You have no one except yourself and perhaps your family to account to."

The interior of the conference room has been hung with fabric so as to create the impression of a field campaign tent. The large screen gives away the role of digital technology in the everyday life of John Simpson Architects. What many people have not yet begun to appreciate is role that modern technology has played in making beauty and tradition a reality once again in the twenty first century.

VI

CONCLUSION

This book, showing the Simpsons at home, has followed the development of his style over more than three decades. There are some constants in the story. While each of the buildings is different, they are all works of three-dimensional geometry, ingenious in their use of space, dramatic in the impression made on guests, full of music, laughter and histories that are likely to be partly, if not wholly invented. We also see an evolution, often related to the commissions received by John's architectural practice. Working on Buckingham Palace encouraged a bolder use of color, seen in the sumptuous reds and plangent yellows of the redecorated Belsize Park. Buckingham Palace, Gonville and Caius, Eton College, Peterhouse all are venerable in their antiquity, and any intervention can only be made after

205

intense thought and study. Such projects nurtured John's sense of history to the point that he now sees it as a fourth dimension, enhancing the experience that architecture gives of the other three. This is an extension of the typically English tradition of the Picturesque, which acknowledges the role played by association and the imagination in aesthetic response. John cites the Acropolis in Athens and the Forum in Rome as places that evolved over long periods of time, forcing architects to take account of what had been built there before. This forced them to scale heights of invention that they might not otherwise have attempted. When building from scratch, as at Harewell, an invented history creates variation, which is not merely random but has its own cause and effect. Architecture—particularly domestic architecture—need not be remorselessly solemn. Leave room for the playfulness of the *jeu d'esprit*.

And we find another strand in these homes that deserves emphasis, because it not only characterizes John's work as an architect but could influence the development of architecture as a whole. This is technology. John is a Classicist and Classicists as a breed are denigrated by their critics as technophobes who can barely tolerate electric lighting, let alone computers. (They perhaps have in mind Sir Albert Richardson, 1880–1964, who used to play the spinet by candlelight, wearing Georgian clothes.)

But we have seen throughout this book of domestic projects that John has been quick to adopt innovation where it can reduce cost and enrich visual effect. The difference between Ashfold House, a work of the 1980s, and the home in Venice, from the 2010s, is not only that, between the two, John matured as an architect, having relaxed and acquired a more profound sense of what it means to live well, but also the development of digital technology has allowed him to do more.

Look at the upholstery. Woven silk is expensive and was used sparingly at Ashfold; commissioning a small run of a bespoke design for a few sofas and chairs would have been inconceivable. But now textiles can be printed to high standard: it makes little difference how much is required. (The technology is similar to that used in photocopiers but with color-fast ink.) Purists may say that the effect is not quite that of the woven material, but it would take a keen eye to spot the difference, without being told. When John and Erica acquired their first flat at Belsize Park, a voile curtain was screen-printed with an anthemion pattern. But the Palazzo Grimani is graced by tablecloths, bedspreads and wallpaper, all created for the purpose to John's designs. Similarly, the cost of carving has tumbled, due to the use of computer-operated machines. The economics lead to unexpected results. For example, it has become cheaper for a fireplace to be machine carved from an expensive single block of marble than hand-carved out of several less costly blocks; and the single block is more luxurious. But marble and stone still come at a price. Fortunately, acceptable substitutes are often at hand. Most people on seeing the coat-of-arms over the front door at Harewell Hall would think it was stone, yet it has really been machine-carved from a kind of plaster and painted with masonry paint. At Ashfold, the bobbles of a cornice were made by taking a cast from a ping pong ball which was then run out many times. Today, far more complicated motifs, constantly varied if necessary, can be produced by 3-D printing.

(above left) Much of the furniture, including the chaise longue shown here, were designed especially for Ashfold House.

(above right) The table for the dining room including the tablecloth were designed and made for Palazzo Grimani. The pattern for the tablecloth was set out and printed using digital technology.

(right) The new Lord Colyton Room at Caius College in Cambridge. The furniture, light fittings, and carpet were designed to be part of the room. Both the chimney piece in Carrara marble and the Nero Marquina urns were designed as part of the room

These developments have not simply allowed the Simpsons to have a lot of fun with decoration, as they seemingly pull ever more flamboyant effects out of their magician's hat. They have the potential to turn what has been the orthodoxy in architecture over the past hundred years on its head. The central tenet of the Modern movement is that the machine aesthetic—clean lines, no ornament—must be the appropriate style for the age because it expresses the most efficient use of progressive technology. But that argument has been exploded by the arrival of digital technology. Le Corbusier wrote *Vers une Architecture* when mass production was reducing the cost of everyday objects, by turning them out in large numbers, all the same. The industrial processes of the time favored simplicity. But that was then. Nowadays, a single artefact can be created for little more than the unit cost of a run of thousands. The most advanced technology of today favors ornament.

This is already understood in the world of historic restoration. At Strawberry Hill, outside London, for example, Horace Walpole's collections have been lost. But recently a posthumous portrait of his parents that Walpole commissioned from John Eccardt has been reproduced by 3-D printing, along with the frame that it filled. This is no mean feat: the frame, which Walpole believed to be by Grinling Gibbons, is a bravura composition of garlands, cupids and birds. The original remains in the Lewis Walpole Library at Yale, but the near miraculous fidelity of the copy makes it difficult to tell the difference.

Architects, though, have been slow to embrace the opportunity. Many prefer to stick with the minimalist look of the twentieth-century Modernism as an aesthetic choice, unaware perhaps that it is no longer as rational as it once seemed. John Simpson, in the houses shown in this book, opens the eyes of the world to a new realm of visual delight. Classicism is not the fuddy-duddy style of arch-conservatives, wanting a return to the era when Britain was still on the gold standard, for whom

(left) The polychromy of the ceiling for the new debating chamber at Eton College in Windsor was facilitated by the using digital technology to design and manufacture the stencils required to paint the decoration.

(above left) The sculpture for the dolphin fountain spout at Harewell hall uses digital technology in the production of the final installation.

(above right) The large dish light fittings for the multipurpose hall and dining room at the new Pipe Partridge Building at Lady Margaret Hall, Oxford, were specially designed for the room and made by Andy Thorton in 2009.

the typewriter was no advance on the quill pen. Instead, it is proudly revealed as the style of the future, as far as technology is concerned. It used to be said that the craft skills necessary to carve capitals and urns were dead—and so Classicism itself would necessarily wither. When this was shown not to be true, the argument shifted: handwork was so expensive that only millionaires could afford it.

Classicism was the preserve of a reactionary elite. We can now see that it is not so exclusive. The doors of this great treasure house of architecture have been flung open. Everyone can help themselves. John's homes are not only a delight for himself, his family and their many guests, but are a harbinger of the joy that is in store for us all, once the revolutionary possibilities of technology have been absorbed.

(above left) The design for the furniture for Palazzo Grimani was inspired by ancient Roman designs. It was made in mahogany by P&S joinery in Suffolk.
(above right) The Caesar chair also made in mahogany by P&S joinery. The fabric was specially designed by John Simpson and digitally printed.
(right) Detail of the bench for The Queen's Gallery, Buckingham Palace.

VII

POSTSCRIPT BY JOHN SIMPSON

Those of you who have reached this far in the book will have realized I am a Classical architect. These values are explicit in the homes I have created for my family and myself, but I believe their importance stretches beyond these personal Arcadias. Classicism, a tradition that goes back to the beginning of time, may not be a familiar language to many architects these days, as most have forgotten how to speak it. But the relevance of a way of building that has been honed over many, many centuries remains critical to the way in which we can resolve the huge challenges facing us in the twenty-first century. How do we build cities and neighborhoods that enrich people's daily experience? How do we meet the demands of sustainability? Thoughtful people are beginning to realize that the answer to such questions does not lie in the current orthodox ideologies that proved such a disaster in the twentieth century but in the ancient wisdom of Classicism. There were few Classicists in the profession when I started work but their number is rising among the younger generation. Other things too have been happening. The Battle of the Styles (between Modern and traditional forms of architecture) has subsided, Classical architecture is being more widely taught in universities and one crucial objection that was often made to the practice of Classicism has been removed: it is no longer too expensive for everyone to enjoy. Let me use the closing pages of the book to expand on these themes.

The new tower on the corner of Vincent Square and Vane Street in Westminster, London. This is part of John Simpson's redevelopment of the old Rochester Row Police Station, an urban design scheme involving four new buildings and the refurbishment of two listed buildings. The plan included a new public sculpture, a herm depicting Priapus, for the square by Alexander Stoddart.

213

We as human beings are social animals. We love our homes, but we also like to live together in close communities which we do in towns and cities. Even in the country, where there are relatively few of us, our houses are clustered together around a green or a common forming a hamlet or village with a church or village hall at its center. Traditionally the role of Classicism has been, as a guide, to give us a helping hand as we erect new buildings so as to ensure that we make them as attractive as we can and arrange them to form pleasant and enjoyable public spaces.

This tradition evolved over countless generations as we gradually discovered what particular characteristics are especially appealing to us and make our buildings beautiful.

Through experience we have learned what materials to use and how to build to make buildings robust so that they mature and age without the need for constant maintenance and repair. This knowledge has subsequently influenced us and our ancestors and has become established as the way we build. Just as the works of Shakespeare and Chaucer are to literature, the treatises of Vitruvius, Palladio and Vignola form part of an accepted canon that has become the Classical tradition in architecture. This is how we have been able to create the many great and wonderful cities such as Rome, Venice, Paris and London. Our Classical tradition has been the basis around which we have been able to cooperate as a society, across many generations, to build these remarkable places and create the environment that we all share. It is the language that we use for building that we have come to understand as a society, just as English is the language we use to speak between ourselves.

It was only in the twentieth century that this tradition was challenged and the safe continuity that it afforded broken. The perception then, particularly amongst the avant-garde socialist-leaning intellectual class, was that the common people, who formed the bulk of the population and still lacked basic essentials such as a decent home were not being served adequately by this tradition. It was considered too elitist and anachronistic, dedicated to creating lasting and attractive buildings and reliant as it was on craft-based skills it was seen as too slow to deliver the mass housing and facilities required. In an effort to satisfy this need, regardless of the consequences, they impatiently turned to industry. The problem was that the technology available at the time was not capable of dealing with the intricacies that our human functional and aesthetic sensibilities demand. It is easy to forget that at the beginning of the twentieth century the technology available was that of the Model T Ford, biplanes and the heavy industry of ocean liners and battleships.

(above) Masterplan for a new settlement at Monks Wood near Braintree in Essex. The Proposal is for a small town of up to 1500 units designed as five mixed-use neighborhoods. The illustration is for Pattiswick, which forms the center of one of the neighborhoods.

(right top) The design is for 380 new apartments and houses for the new English neighborhood at Val D'Europe at Marne la Vallee outside Paris, France. The client stipulated that they were looking for 'Nash-like' stucco buildings similar to those at Regent's Park in London.

(right bottom) Dickens Heath, a new mixed-use settlement designed by John Simpson. View of the center of Dicken's Heath near Solihull in Birmingham. John Simpson designed the masterplan for Dickens Heath, a new standalone mixed-use settlement acting for Solihull Metropolitan Council. Many of the commercial and public buildings in the center were designed by the practice.

Unfortunately, it is only now, one hundred years later, that we have come to realize the devastating consequences this approach has had on brutalising our cities and the environment in which we live. It has been catastrophic on our mental health and well-being as a society and, in addition, this over reliance on industry has contributed to the depletion of natural resources and the widespread pollution and global warming that is threatening our planet today.

This realization has brought about significant changes in attitude and as we move into the twenty-first century, technology and what it can deliver has moved a long way and particularly so with regard to building. In construction, computer-based technology is just beginning to come of age with digital scanning, virtual modeling, 3-D printing and CNC machines that can carve materials such as stone and wood. Colorfast printing can now be done at relatively large scale onto materials such as fabrics, wallpapers and ceramics. This has already created a sea change in architecture where detail and complexity, only possible before using craft-based techniques, is becoming economical and this is without taking into account the additional benefits that robotics technology is likely to bring to construction. One of the consequences of this change is that the economics of production is not reliant anymore on the large-scale repetition that the old industrial processes demanded. This technology is responsive to great intricacy and detail, too, and can be used economically in individual bespoke production. Unlike the old industrial techniques, it is no more the enemy of tradition. We can now use technology for construction without having to live in a concrete jungle. It is, in fact, technology itself that is capable of giving us back our pride as human beings so that we can all enjoy our built tradition, our homes and our cities once again.

Bespoke wallpaper designs for the Biedermeier Room *(left)* and the Pompeiian Bedroom *(right)* at Palazzo Grimani in Venice and for the main hall and gallery *(center)* at Harewell Hall, Wherwell, Hampshire.

One of the major challenges of the twenty-first century is the pressure to create scores of new cities, and the expansion of existing ones. The United Nations is predicting that around the world we shall need to house a predicted global population of ten billion by 2050. This is far greater than anything we faced in the twentieth century. There is nevertheless still a long way to go before this new technology is going to be able to cope with this challenge. I hope that the work illustrated in this book has given you a glimpse of what is possible and shown you that the foundations have already been laid. I am confident that as the century wears on we shall increasingly have the means to do what we need to do and this time to do it successfully so that the failures of the twentieth century are not repeated once more. If we are to save humanity and the ecology of the planet, our greatest obstacle will not be technology but the time needed for its results to take effect.

ACKNOWLEDGMENTS

I would like to thank my wife, Erica, for being so patient and putting up with the many alterations, modifications and changes in our homes which, at times, must have seemed never ending. Without her advice, encouragement and help in decorating, furnishing and establishing each as a practical and comfortable place to live, these projects would not have resulted in the beautiful and enjoyable homes where we have been able to bring up our children and entertain our friends. Erica also carried out the vital role of keeping expenditure under control, which, as anyone familiar with building at home knows, can prove especially challenging at times! To our boys, Nicholas and Alexander, and our daughter, Antonia, a special thanks, too, for being such patient guinea pigs, testing out ideas which in some cases must have seemed somewhat trying. I do hope that, at least in part, this venture of house building did prove enjoyable and exciting with features such as having bunk beds designed into a little house of your own within the nursery bedroom. Thank you, too, for helping entertain our friends, when they came to see us, with your remarkable capacity for music making when they came to see us, and especially so at the Christmas parties that we have always held at Belsize Park. To my parents, John and Lydia, for starting this process off and for having the trust and confidence to commission me to design Ashfold House at a time when I had so very little experience, having just graduated from architecture school. To my brother, Michael, who was invaluable supervising the construction on site and for the extraordinary care and attention to detail he put into getting Ashfold built and in the construction and renovation of the works at Great James Street. I would also like to thank my fellow director at the practice, Joanna Wachowiak, for helping make these designs become a reality and on whom I have increasingly come to rely. She is supported by an ever-increasing team in the office, led by Tiffany Abernathy, with her characteristic boundless energy and infectious enthusiasm, and by Victoria Landeryou, with her remarkable capacity for organization and detail.

221

Looking across the upper landing of the stair hall at the Queen's Gallery, Buckingham Palace, showing scagliola columns and mahogany doors. The balustrade of the stair is a reference to a stair at the Altes Museum built from 1825–1830 in Berlin, which Leo Von Klenze also references in his design for the Hermitage in St. Petersburg in 1838. Both buildings are museums designed to house royal collections.

There have also been a number of people in the practice whom I would like to mention; people who have contributed so much over the years, and been particularly associated with the projects illustrated in this book. Peter Powlesland, for the exceptional care and energy he put into developing the details for Ashfold House, Great James Street and Belsize Park. I am also grateful to Richard Economakis, for his work detailing the furniture at Belsize Park and also for the design of our wedding cake incorporating the orders of architecture. To Ettore Brunetti for helping to get Palazzo Grimani designed and detailed, and in dealing with the remarkably byzantine system of approvals in Italy, and also to Peter Walker who supervised and directed the all-important finishing touches at the palazzo. Peter was also instrumental in getting the project at Harewell Hall done and was involved in the project from inception and planning through to completion. I am particularly grateful to him for the dedication he put into getting all the detail just right. I would like to thank Ettore, too, for his work on the computer and as an artist in developing the various wallpaper patterns, especially those using false perspective, which we used to great effect at Palazzo Grimani and at Harewell Hall. I would also like to thank Rena Multaputri, for her work on the furniture and for developing the digital patterns for the fabrics used on both projects.

I would like to thank Clive Aslet for bringing these projects to life in this book with his remarkable text and the photographers June Buck, Colin Dutton, Dylan Thomas and Will Pryce . . . and especially Andreas von Einsiedel, without whose eye for detail and composition these projects could never have been brought to you in such a vibrant and exciting way.

Last but not least are all the friends such as the late Professor David Watkin, Clive Aslet, Paul Doyle, Marcus Binney, Demetri Porphyrios, Leon Krier, Sandy Stoddart and the many others for their support and encouragement over the years.

—J. S.

Watercolor showing the north elevation to the new west wing at Buckhurst Park by John Simpson. Built for the late King Hussein of Jordan at Ascot near Windsor in England. The project involved two new extensions and the refurbishment of an existing building. The new extensions were built in stucco with Portland stone dressings and a welsh slate roof.

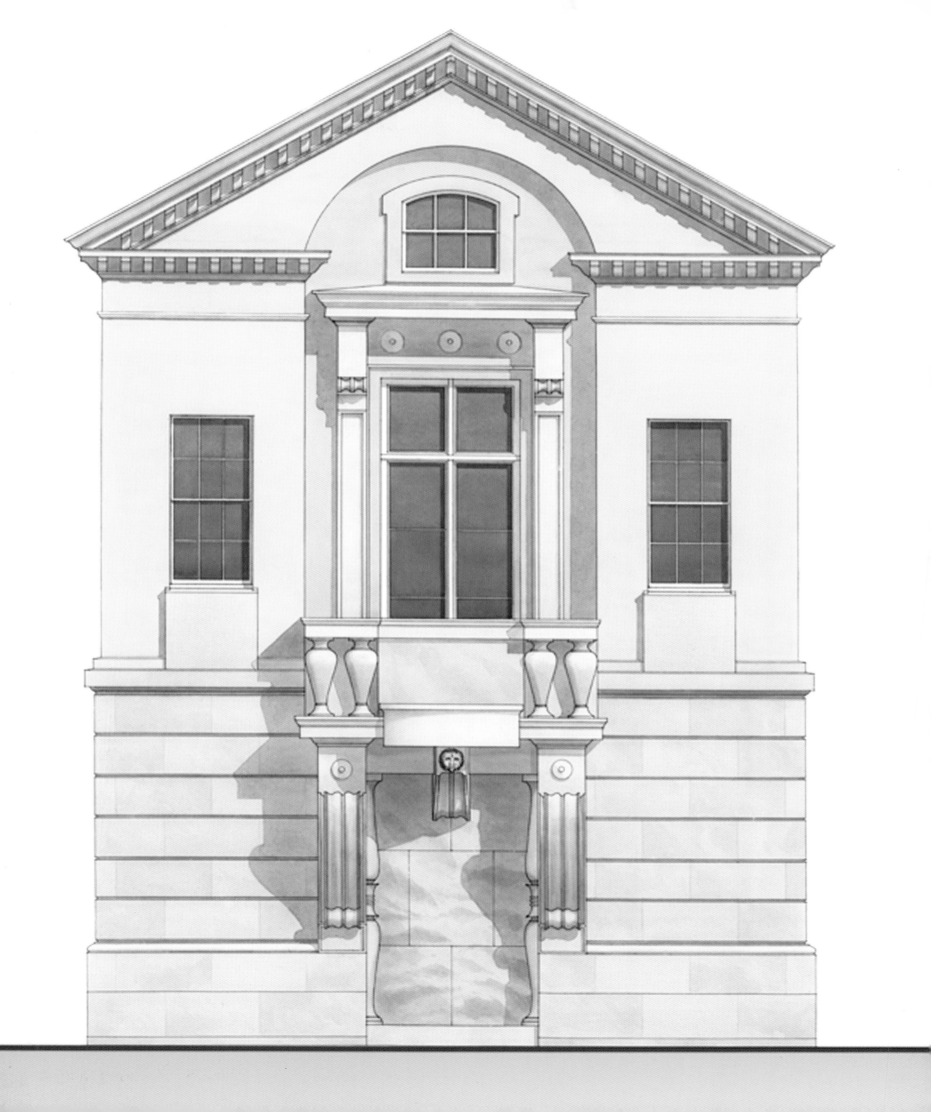

(front endpapers) Fabric patterns for furniture upholstery, designed by John Simpson and used at Palazzo Grimani in Venice and Harewell Hall in Hampshire; fabric pattern designed to cover 12 dining chairs at Palazzo Grimani (opposite page 1). Designing bespoke patterns runs on such a small scale it would have been prohibitively costly before the advent of digital technology.

(back endpapers) Tablecloth fabric design, Palazzo Grimani (opposite page 224); Door panel design, Palazzo Grimani.

(page 2) Watercolor (end of terrace elevation) for a house at Knokke Heist in Belgium by John Simpson. This is part of a commercial development for a new settlement. It is designed picking up on the traditional vernacular of buildings in the area using buff brick and a red tiled roof.

(pages 6–7) Proposal for a memorial for troops from the Commonwealth who died during the World Wars located at Constitutional Hill at Hyde Park. The proposed gate piers frame the view of the existing arch by Decimus Burton built in 1826 and moved to its current location in 1882–1883. The proposal involved the removal of the Quadriga that surmounts the arch and replacing it so that it faces the new gates on Constitution Hill. (Watercolor by Alexander Creswell.)

(pages 12–13) Capriccio showing the new buildings at the McCrum Yard development at Eton College, Windsor, designed by John Simpson. These include three new departmental buildings for Modern Languages, Theology and Philosophy and Politics and Economics, a new museum for Egyptian and Classical antiquities and a new debating chamber attached to the School of Politics. (Painting by Carl Laubin.)

(pages 26–27) Design for the new buildings at London Bridge City in Southwark London by John Simpson. View of the development from the Tower of London. It is designed around a new square overlooking the Thames providing a mix of uses including office and retail. (Painting by Carl Laubin.)

(pages 218–219) The Defence and National Rehabilitation Centre designed by John Simpson puts patients in an environment that is familiar and attractive, that which promotes feelings of contentment and aids the process of medical recovery. Historically, this approach was commonly used as a medical tool and can be seen in the way old monastic infirmaries and early hospitals were arranged around pleasant courts with arcades and cloisters forming a safe sanctuary of peace and tranquility. (Painting by Carl Laubin.)

Image Credits:
© Colin Dutton /Sotheby's: front cover, 28, 31, 34-75, 206 (right);
© John Simpson Architects: 2, 6-7 (watercolor by Alexander Creswell), 8 (painting by Carl Laubin), 10, 11, 12-13 (painting by Carl Laubin), 18-21, 22 (left), 23, 25, 26, 27 (painting by Carl Laubin), 33, 78-81, 90, 91, 94-97, 102, 109, 114, 116-117, 126-129, 150-157, 161-169, 172-175, 179-185, 188 (painting by Ed Venn), 189, 206 (left), 207, 210, 214, 215 (top), 216, 217-218 (painting by Carl Laubin), 223; © 2021 Jonathan Wallen: 14; © Creative Commons: 16; © Wikimedia Commons: 17, 30; © Andreas von Einsiedel: 22 (right), 76, 82-89, 92-93, 98-101, 104-107, 110, 186, 190-202, 209 (right): Royal Collection Trust / © Her Majesty Queen Elizabeth II 2021: 23, 24, 204, 214, 220; © Dylan Thomas: 112, 118-125, 136-137, 140, 142-145, 149, 209 (left), back cover: © Will Pryce/Country Life/Future Publishing Ltd.: 130-131, 134-135, 138-139, 147, 148; © June Buck/Country Life/Future Publishing Ltd: 158-159, 170-171, 176; © Sarah J Duncan Photography: 212; © Rick McEvoy Photography: 215 (bottom)

First published in the United States of America in 2021 by
RIZZOLI INTERNATIONAL PUBLICATIONS, INC.
300 Park Avenue South, New York, NY 10010
www.rizzoliusa.com

© 2021 Rizzoli International Publications, Inc.
© 2021 John Simpson

Publisher: Charles Miers
Editor: Douglas Curran
Production Manager: Colin Hough Trapp
Managing Editor: Lynn Scrabis

Designed by Takaaki Matsumoto, Matsumoto Inc.
Assisted by Robin Brunelle, Amy Wilkins

Printed and bound in China

2021 2022 2023 2024 2025/ 10 9 8 7 6 5 4 3 2 1

ISBN-13: 978-0-8478-7063-9
Library of Congress Control Number: 2021937394

Visit us online:
Facebook.com/RizzoliNewYork
Twitter: @Rizzoli_Books
Instagram.com/RizzoliBooks
Pinterest.com/RizzoliBooks
Youtube.com/user/RizzoliNY
Issuu.com/Rizzoli